"Michael Card is both a wonderful artist and a serious scholar. Such a marriage of two souls with one pen in his delicate but honest hand is glorious. Every sentence in *A Better Freedom* is a learning experience and an act of worship. At the end of every paragraph one runs into an altar and a gallery. Christ is both honored and reverenced. I read and reflected, I contemplated my own freedom, and realized that only when I pursue spiritual submission do I secure my place in God's affirmation. 'Well done, thou good and perfect slave' is the sign posted above the shortest way to glory."

CALVIN MILLER, *Beeson Divinity School, author of* The Singer and The Path of Celtic Prayer

"I am thrilled that Michael Card has taken on the challenge of writing about the slave-master relationship as it relates to us (Christians) as slaves and Christ our Master. Historically from the African American perspective, being slaves has had a negative connotation. Michael's book deals with that, but at the same time points us to a biblical reality: if we saw ourselves as slaves to Christ our Master, how much more we could do as members of his body! What a wonderful body of Christ we would be if each of us saw Christ as our Master. It is time to trade in our old paradigms and accept the wonderful reality that we are all slaves to Christ and he is our Master! All those who read Michael's book will be challenged to rethink who we are in Christ!"

DR. DOLPHUS WEARY, *president, R.E.A.L. Christian Foundation; president emeritus, Mission Mississippi; former president, The Mendenhall Ministries; and author of* I Ain't Comin' Back

"This is an unusual, rigorous but conversational Bible study tuned to a vivid presentation of Roman and African American slavery. Its storybook character, under Michael Card's genial historical insight and gentle spirit, issues a compelling picture of our calling to be faithful slaves today of the merciful Master, Jesus Christ."

CALVIN SEERVELD, *emeritus, Institute for Christian Studies, Toronto*

"This is Mike Card at his best. Through his prophetic voice as an artist he has once again done a great service. In a world filled with confining, imprisoning self-indulgence, Card recaptures and challenges us to hear the biblical word for servant as it should be. To be a *servant* is to be Christ's slave. It is simple and complex—easy to say, profound to follow. It, the gospel, is a better freedom."

REV. SCOTT ROLEY, *senior pastor, Christ Community Church, Franklin, Tennessee, and coauthor of* God's Neighborhood

"When I read any book by Michael Card, I know the ideas have been thoroughly wrested, personally, academically, biblically and poetically from every source. Like many of the contextual references in the Bible, slavery can be difficult for me to understand as having anything to do with my Christianity. But for Paul it was the metaphor of choice to describe his new freedom. *A Better Freedom* explores this kingdom mystery of what it means to be truly free."

SARA GROVES, *singer/songwriter*

Michael Card

A BETTER FREEDOM

Finding Life as Slaves of Christ

A better freedom can't be found
by those unwilling to be bound.
A better freedom is not known
by those whose hearts will not
be owned. But those who follow
find a better freedom.

≋
IVP Books
An imprint of InterVarsity Press
Downers Grove, Illinois

InterVarsity Press
P.O. Box 1400, Downers Grove, IL 60515-1426
World Wide Web: www.ivpress.com
E-mail: email@ivpress.com

InterVarsity Press® is the book-publishing division of InterVarsity Christian Fellowship/USA®,
a student movement active on campus at hundreds of universities, colleges and schools of nursing in
the United States of America, and a member movement of the International Fellowship of Evangelical
Students. For information about local and regional activities, write Public Relations Dept.,
InterVarsity Christian Fellowship/USA, 6400 Schroeder Rd., P.O. Box 7895, Madison, WI
53707-7895, or visit the IVCF website at <www.intervarsity.org>.

Design: Cindy Kiple
Images: ball and chain: Dusty Cline/iStockphoto
　　　　grungy paper: ranplett/iStockphoto

ISBN 978-0-8308-3714-4

Library of Congress Cataloging-in-Publication Data

Card, Michael, 1957-
　A better freedom: finding life as slaves of Christ/Michael Card.
　　p.cm.
　Includes bibliographical references.
　ISBN 978-0-8308-3714-4 (pbk.: alk. paper)
　1. Spirituality. 2. Christian life. I. Title.
　BV4501.3.C3665 2009
　270.086'25—dc22
　　　　　　　　2009021598

P　20　19　18　17　16　15　14　13　12　11　10　9　8　7　6　5　4　3　2　1

Y　25　24　23　22　21　20　19　18　17　16　15　14　13　12　11　10　09

This book is dedicated

with deep gratitude to Ron Davis.

If you had not enfleshed so effortlessly

all the ideas in this book

about selfless servanthood,

I would have never been able

to imagine them.

Contents

A Better Freedom

Christ revealed himself to me
Enslaved my soul to set me free
I was bound to at him at Calvary
And found a better freedom

That Soul who suffered in the dark
Has purchased and unchained my heart
A shining slavery did impart
To find a better freedom

A better freedom can't be found
By those unwilling to be bound
A better freedom is not known
By those whose hearts will not be owned
But those who follow find a better freedom

We never can be truly free
Till we're bound to this community
The Incarnation lets us see
A path to better freedom

A slave to sin, my heart before
Was bolted like a prison door
But in slavery to the Risen Lord
I found a better freedom

A better freedom can't be found
By those unwilling to be bound
A better freedom is not known
By those whose hearts will not be owned
But those who follow find a better freedom

Come with him and find a better freedom
Follow me and find a better freedom

Music and lyrics by Scott Roley and Michael Card
(Recording available for free download at <michaelcard.com>)

Introduction

There the conviction was suddenly borne in upon me that Christianity is preeminently the religion of slaves, that slaves cannot help belonging to it, and I among others.

SIMONE WEIL

IN ORDER TO BE TRULY FREE one must become a slave to Christ.

This book comes from a paradox. Basing books on paradoxes is risky enough, but when the paradox is centered on a corrupt institution as complex and convoluted as slavery you are really asking for trouble. But Jesus was always asking for trouble, and he is forever redeeming things that are corrupted and convoluted.

This book has been rewritten many times. It began as a novel about a first-century slave. The slave was named Apolumius. He was owned by a Jewish merchant who had rescued him as an infant from a garbage dump. Together the two men journeyed to the ancient city of Ephesus, where they met the elderly apostle John. Along the way I took every imaginable opportunity to talk about the life of a slave from the New Testament era. Those who read that first rough manuscript of the novel agreed that the story was far more about the intricacies of slavery than the characters or the plot. They were correct. The novel was a failure. Who wants to be a novelist anyway?

So I started again, focusing simply on slavery, with no characters and no story. But this version didn't come together either. There was still something missing. I had failed to include the force that had drawn me to the topic of slavery in the New Testament in the first place—the experience of African American slaves. Having been a part of two African American congregations, I had heard my brothers and sisters speak almost continually of Jesus as their "Master." They were able to relate to him in a way that had been closed to me. I needed to include, as best I could, their illuminating perspective. The result is the book you now hold in your hands.

What This Is and What It Is Not

This book is meant to provide a basic introduction to the subject of slavery, in both biblical and modern times, and what it means for the Christian life. It is designed to foster an interest in the topic. I hope that it will get you hooked on the notion of the radical transformation that occurs when someone embraces the gospel as a servant. It is about how freedom comes from slavery.

The book does not pretend to be a comprehensive statement on first-century slavery, a broad and deep topic that has called forth shelves of books. It does not intend to argue for the use of the word *slave* over and above the word *servant*. The issue is a matter not of translation but transformation. For those who want to dig deeper into the academic issues a bibliography has been provided. In regard to slavery in the New Testament, I suggest you begin with Murray J. Harris's *Slave of Christ*, a wonderfully concise yet comprehensive book on the subject.

Neither does this book pretend to be anything like a complete introduction to the African American slave experience. For every book on first-century slavery I would guess there are a hundred on slavery in America. The voices of African American slaves appear in this book to speak for those first-century slaves who have no voice, who left virtually no record. To hear more of their voices, see the bibliography in the back. I would encourage you to begin with either Henry Louis Gates's *The Classic Slave Narratives* or the truly amazing collection by Kai Wright, *The African American Archive.*

It is also beyond the scope of this book to adequately discuss the current crisis of slavery in our time. The unthinkable truth is that there are more men and women, boys and girls enslaved in the world today than in the three centuries of African American slavery combined! I have included in appendix E a brief overview of the facts of modern-day slavery. My hope is that in the process of reading this book and engaging with the topic, your heart will be stirred to the global calamity that is human slavery. Sara Groves, a dear sister and fellow writer and musician, has provided a coda, a final note, reflecting on her exposure to human trafficking today. I hope that once we begin to reclaim our place alongside Christ as his slaves, we will take up the cause of those tens of millions throughout the world who are still in chains today.

AT THE LEVEL OF THE IMAGINATION

I will never forget the morning thirty years ago when William Lane looked over his glasses at me and said, "I am going to teach you how I read Scripture." It seemed an unusual thing to say; after all, I could read. But in the years that followed, I slowly learned what it was he was talking about, how he "read" Scripture. He referred to it as "interacting at the level of the imagination," and it will be my standard approach throughout this book as we wrestle with the biblical notion of slavery.

To read at the level of the imagination is to seek to understand with the heart as well as the mind. It involves putting yourself in the place of those who first heard the words of the text. Bill liked to stress that we must interact by means of the "*informed* imagination." Which is to say that we must do our homework before coming to the text of Scripture by becoming familiar with first-century resources and wrestling with the original languages if need be. Only the informed imagination can listen responsibly and imaginatively. Otherwise we simply speculate, with no connection to the real-life situation of the original hearers of the text.

Finally, be reminded that even though the focus of our discussion is slavery, this is fundamentally a book about freedom; what it means and the only way to ultimately find it. The early Christians found freedom by becoming slaves to Christ. How is that possible?

Though being "in very nature God," Jesus came in the form of a slave. Why?

How is it that early Christianity was regarded as a slave religion?

Why did some of the first followers of Jesus sell themselves into slavery in order to set others free?

How could Africans, who neither spoke nor read the language of their captors, who were persecuted and kept in chains by a nation that called itself Christian, nevertheless come to Jesus en masse?

If we can cross that bridge between the heart and mind, and wrestle with some of these difficult passages at the level of the imagination, we just might be able to find the answers to these questions, and more.

PART ONE

BEGINNING
A JOURNEY

1

My Master

THE SILENCE HAD JUST SETTLED IN, a warm blanket, enveloping the congregation. Huddled beneath the comfort of that silence, my eyes were shut tight. Though the stillness was familiar, little else that morning was, for this was not "my" church. I was aware of the creaking of the ancient floors, the groaning of the pews, the musty smell of almost two centuries, for that is how long a worshiping community had been coming here for prayer. How many nervous couples had stood at the end of this aisle, waiting to hear the words "You are now man and wife"? How many coffins had rested there while a congregation lamented?

The padding on the pew seemed thin as I rested my right hand on the coarse material. All at once, a large, warm hand took hold of my left. Through one squinting eye I peeked over to see who it was. I would come to know her as Dinah, Bob's wife. Together the two of them had raised or fostered over seventy-five children, black and white. That morning, without knowing it, I began to be adopted. "If I don't love them, I don't know who else will!" was Dinah's only rationale for decades of such extravagant loving. Though I was a stranger, I sensed her no-nonsense acceptance and affection for me. Without knowing it, I had entered a world full of such surprises there at the First Missionary Baptist Church.

All around, prayers were being offered up; unfamiliar, repeated prayer formulas echoed through the congregation. I heard combinations of words and thoughts that had never occurred to me:

"I thank you for *the full use of my limbs* . . ."

". . . that I awoke this morning *from the very image of death* . . ."

(A sprinkling of Amens and Oh, yeses.)

"I give thanks for *waking up in my right mind.*"

"Sweet Jesus, *there was food in my cupboard* this morning. We do not take this for granted."

"Yes, Lord," Dinah whispered under her breath, giving my hand a squeeze.

As the time of corporate prayer came to an end, Denny, the pastor, stood up to offer his closing words. I had prayed with Denny for years at a separate weekly prayer gathering and had heard what he was about to say a thousand times. Yet this morning, surrounded by this African American congregation, I heard it for the first time. "*My Master*, strong God . . ." he intoned.

Our most important journeys begin before we know we have taken a step. That morning a dozen years ago, this particular journey began for me. I, the sole representative of the dominant and usually domineering culture, was warmly welcomed by everyone, including the elderly woman who honestly yet kindly asked, "What are *you* doing here anyway?" By coming I had hoped to show my solidarity with Denny, with a group of us, red, black and white, who were committed to racial reconciliation in our town. We had been trying to attract African Americans to our congregation for years. One day it occurred to me, *Why don't we go to them?*

Without knowing it, I had placed myself on a path toward a new understanding of Jesus of Nazareth. The implications were so far reaching that I am still struggling to understand them. I had begun a journey to a new solidarity with him, my Master and Servant Savior.

"Master . . ." I had never in my long Christian life heard Jesus referred to by that title. But in the context of an African American church service it struck me with disturbing clarity. When I asked Denny later, he confirmed, "Slaves generally referred to Jesus as 'Master' to let their earthly masters know they *weren't*."

The tragic fact of their bondage nevertheless provided slaves with a unique ability to connect with Jesus, which they did by the hundreds of thousands. I saw as never before the potential meaning the slave experience has for the contemporary church, both black and white, which so badly needs to rediscover what it means to submit to Jesus as Master. I wondered what it would mean to become, in the true New Testament sense, his slaves.

So I began asking questions. What did it mean for African American slaves to acknowledge Jesus as Master? What did Paul, Peter, Jude and James mean when they acknowledged themselves as Christ's slaves? What could it mean for me to join my brothers and sisters by affirming that Jesus is my Master? What would it mean for us all to deliberately take upon ourselves the title "slave of Christ"?

Those questions sent me on a journey that began in the Old Testament, as I sought to understand the initial slave experience and identity of Israel. Next, in the New Testament, I listened in a fresh way to the words of Paul, who, after all, identified himself more than once as a "slave of Christ Jesus." Finally, I fled to the life of the Servant Savior. I listened all over again to parables I thought I had squeezed dry long ago. To my surprise, I discovered how frequently Jesus appealed to the image of slaves in his luminous stories, how often he set them up as exemplars.

All along this journey I read and listened to the narratives of African American slaves, to their articulate accounts of what it cost, of what it meant to be a slave. They became my companions along the way. Their whispered accounts of submission and suffering, of radical obedience and miraculous forbearance, shed new light on the words of the Bible.

I invite you to join me on this journey of discovery, to become acquainted with the complex and contradictory world of slavery, to listen to what the Scriptures tell us at the level of the imagination, to seek to listen to the word with both the heart and mind as they can only be integrated by the imagination. Most especially, come flee to the life of Jesus, who came in the form of a servant, who lived as a slave, but who is nevertheless our "Master and strong God."

The world seduces us with slavery and calls it freedom. Christ calls us to become his slaves, to take up the easy yoke, which is the only freedom.

2

A Better Freedom

But let slaves serve the more faithfully to the glory of God, that they may obtain a better freedom from God.

IGNATIUS
LETTER TO POLYCARP 4.3 (A.D. 110)

IF IT IS TRUE THAT THE PROSPECT OF DEATH marvelously focuses the mind, then no one's mind was ever clearer than Ignatius's as he made his final journey to Rome and death in the arena. He had been a disciple of John, appointed the second bishop of Antioch in A.D. 69. (Paul had only just been martyred in A.D. 64.) Paul's epistles had been written during Ignatius's lifetime. He is the first Christian writer after Paul. Ignatius is as far back as we can go in the history of the church without actually stepping back onto the stage of the New Testament itself.

As the second century was dawning, Ignatius was caught up in one of the first waves of persecution of the followers of Jesus. Having been found guilty, he was sentenced to "fight the wild beasts" in the amphitheater. What little we know of him we learn from the sparse details of this final journey from Antioch to Rome in A.D. 110, during the reign of Trajan.

Eusebius, the first historian of the church, tells us that during an extended rest stop outside the city of Smyrna, Ignatius wrote five letters to the churches of Ephesus, Magnesia, Tralles, Philadelphia and Smyrna. Outside the city he was met by a small delegation made up of Polycarp, the bishop of Smyrna, and two other men. Polycarp, who had also been a disciple of John, would later become one of the most celebrated martyrs in the history of the early church. Ignatius dictated the final letters to the second man in the group, a scribe named Burrhus. He closed his letter to Smyrna with these words:

> I salute the bishop, worthy of God, and the presbytery, fit for God, and my fellow slaves. (12.3)

The man who spoke these words, on his way to die, had let go of his rights, knowing that a slave has none. He had sacrificed his identity, finding a new one in his Master, Jesus. To see him sitting beside the road chained to two Roman soldiers (he refers to them as "leopards"), you would assume he was only a slave. He saw himself as "wheat to be ground in the teeth of wild beasts." As a faithful servant, his final hope would have been to hear, "Well done, my good and faithful *slave*," when at long last the grinding pain was over.

It is all the hope he needs for now. His self-understanding as a slave of Christ gave Ignatius a disturbing clarity, just as it had done for John, Peter, Paul, James, Jude and even Mary. Having let go of everything else, Ignatius held onto the One, to Jesus, who was also known as a slave.

In an earlier letter to his friend Polycarp, Ignatius had warned the slaves in the church at Smyrna not to become impatient and discontent because of the fact that the church had not yet purchased their freedom. He wrote, "Offer a more devoted service so that you may obtain from God a better freedom." He wanted the followers of Jesus in Smyrna to understand that their choice was not between slavery and freedom. The choice has always only been whose slave you will be. As Jesus had offered wisdom through foolishness, maturity through childlikeness, and wealth through poverty, Ignatius understood that the only way to this "better freedom" was to be found in slavery to Christ.

When the last letter was finished, Burrhus the scribe rolled it up and handed it to the third member of the farewell delegation. He was the bishop of the great church of Ephesus, having succeeded John himself. His name was Onesimus, the runaway slave on whose behalf Paul had written to Philemon.

Of all the confusion and anguish the small delegation must have felt as they watched Ignatius stumbling away in chains to a certain and violent death, one thing was clear to them all. This was a man who had found a better freedom.

"Take up your cross and follow me." These are slave words from Jesus, for crucifixion was a slave's death (Matthew 10:38; 16:24). Come into a new, unimaginable way of life. Leave one way of thinking and living behind and enter into the mystery of an unimaginable new reality.

"Take up my yoke," Jesus invites. Take your place alongside others who are slaving for me and for the gospel. Take up the basin and the towel. Wash feet with the water of my Word. Let go of all your expectations, of the illusion that you possess "rights." Abandon the myth of freedom the world offers and come find a better freedom. It is the only freedom you will ever know in an unfree world. They are parallels; the cross and the yoke of slavery. Jesus bids us pick them both up.

Like the cross, slavery is both paradigm and paradox. The cross, the most excruciating and pervasive symbol of suffering and death in the first century, has come to represent for the followers of Jesus the only way to peace and life. In the same sense slavery, which represents the total denial of freedom, becomes for the follower of Christ, the Servant Savior, the only means to the realization of the true freedom, which Ignatius in his letter to Polycarp called a "better freedom." The basin, the towel, the yoke and the cross; the implements of grace Jesus offers. They are the very tools he himself used. He came in the form of a slave, not to offer us freedom from slavery but a new kind of slavery that is freedom.

In order to become rich you must become poor (Luke 12:33). In order to become mature you must rediscover your own childlikeness (Mark 9:36). In order to become wise you must embrace the foolishness of the gospel (1 Corinthians 3:18). In Jesus, life comes through death (John 5:24) and the only true freedom comes from slavery to him (1 Corinthians 7:22). He came to turn the world upside down, to shatter all our definitions and images, and to fulfill them. The fundamental mysteries of following Jesus are always rooted in paradox.

These are the harsh realities of faith in Jesus. If we are to be his followers in the truest biblical sense, we must give ourselves to understanding them.

3

One Word, Three Worlds

WORLDS COME TOGETHER IN WORDS when you read Scripture at the level of the imagination. The word *slave* calls together at least three worlds; the Old Testament Hebrew world, the New Testament Roman world and for us, the world of the African American slave. The resonances of these disparate worlds accounts for the complexity involved in recapturing the biblical meaning of the word *slave*. Whenever Peter or perhaps Paul speaks of slavery, their thoughts originate from their unique background in Judaism, yet they speak into their contemporary world, defined by Roman slavery. But finally, their words fall on our ears, which have been conditioned to imagine slavery in our own milieu. One word is spoken, three worlds come together. (See appendix A.)

THE OLD TESTAMENT WORLD OF SLAVERY

A son honors [his] father, and a servant *[ebed]* his master. But if I am a father, where is My honor? And if I am a master, where is [your] fear of Me? says the LORD of Hosts to you priests, who despise My name. (Malachi 1:6)

From the very beginning the national identity of Israel was connected to slavery. In what amounts to the preamble to the Ten Commandments, God reminds his people, "I am the LORD your

God, who brought you out of the land of Egypt, *out of the place of slavery*" (Exodus 20:2). The very first block of legal mandates that precede the Decalogue has to do with the protection of slaves. Later in Deuteronomy 5:15 when the Ten Commandments are recited once more, God commands the people to remember the sabbath and to extend its sacred rest even to male and female slaves. They are to show such kindness because "you were a slave in the land of Egypt." And in Leviticus 25:42, the reason God gives for forbidding that his people be sold as slaves is not that they are supposed to be free, but rather that they are his slaves.

For four centuries, from Joseph to Moses, God's people had lived as slaves in Egypt. In the world of the Old Testament, "slave of the LORD" was a title of honor. In the Old Testament Abraham, David, Moses and Joshua are all referred to by the Hebrew word for slave *(ebed)*. Though, slavery played only a minimal role in Jewish society, the Jews were the kindest of slaveholders in the ancient world. Jewish slavery was often so benign that a special provision was made for slaves who, after their time of servitude expired, chose to remain slaves. It has been called the "order of the pierced ear." Exodus 21:5-6 states:

> But if the slave declares: "I love my master, my wife, and my children; I do not want to leave as a free man," his master is to bring him to the judges and then bring him to the door or doorpost. His master must pierce his ear with an awl, and he will serve his master for life.

In the second division of the Old Testament, the Wisdom Writings, there are two central characters, Job and David. Both men are characterized as slaves. God always defines Job as "my servant" (Job 1:8; 2:3; 42:7, 8). And in the Psalter David becomes the paradigm for the term. In the superscriptions to Psalms 18 and 36, he or whoever might have added the titles identifies him as "David, the servant of the Lord." In psalm after psalm the relationship between the Lord and his faithful slaves is hammered out:

The Master delights in the well-being of his slave. (35:27)

He will save him. (86:2)

He gives him great joy. (86:4)

He provides strength. (86:16)

He does him good. (119:17)

He teaches his servant. (119:35)

He keeps his promises to him. (119:38)

He will deliver him. (144:10)

Meanwhile the slave of the Lord pleads with him (27:9; 69:17), rejoices because of him (109:28) and finally pledges his servanthood (116:16).

When we come to the third and final division of the Old Testament, the Prophets, we find the same preoccupation with the idea of the faithful slave. Isaiah and Daniel are both directly referred to by the term (Isaiah 20:3; Daniel 6:20). One of the most frequent epithets is "my servants [ebed] the prophets" (Jeremiah 7:25; 25:4; 29:19; 44:4; Ezra 9:11; Ezekiel 38:17; Daniel 9:6, 10; Amos 3:7; Zechariah 1:6).

But in the prophets the term *slave* is primarily a messianic designation. It is "the most prominent personal, technical term to represent the Old Testament teaching on the Messiah." The central core of this teaching is found in the last twenty-seven chapters of Isaiah. In the prophets, it might be said, the name for the Messiah is "slave."

> Here is my servant *[ebed]*, whom I uphold,
> my chosen one in whom I delight;
> I will put my Spirit on him
> and he will bring justice to the nations. (Isaiah 42:1 NIV)

Though benign by comparison, even in Old Testament slavery one person was owned by another and abuse was invariably still a reality. The prime example is the abuse of Hagar by her mistress Sarai in Genesis 16. Due to her own apparent infertility and refusal to believe the unbelievable promise that she would be a mother, Sarai gives to Abram her slave Hagar. The slave girl obeys her mistress and submits her body to become the surrogate for Sarai. When she gives birth to a son, Ishmael, Sarai becomes jealous and persecutes Hagar, who eventually flees into the wilderness with her son. In the wilderness the runaway slave becomes the recipient of special revelation and comes to know the Lord by a special name she herself gives to him, "El Roi," the "God of Seeing." Even this early in the story of salvation, God is recognized as the One who sees, hears and rescues slaves.

SLAVERY IN THE NEW TESTAMENT WORLD

> It is singularly monstrous that ancient Rome should be praised for having bequeathed to us the notion of rights. If we examine Roman law in its cradle, to see what species it belongs to, we discover that . . . in fact the things which the property owner had the right to use or abuse at will were for the most part human beings. (Simone Weil)

When we enter the New Testament, we encounter a completely different world of slavery. The reason, put simply, is Rome. For most of its 982-year existence, the economy of Rome was heavily (some scholars say completely) dependent on slave labor. Early in its history, Rome's many wars of conquest yielded millions of captives. Those captives were sold into slavery, which Dionysius of Halicarnassus referred to as "the most just means" since it was considered more humane to enslave captives rather than to execute them. This rationale gave shape to the Roman mindset toward slavery for centuries. The slave owner could always justify his ownership of another human being by saying, "We might have executed you in battle. Instead we graciously allowed you to go on living." By this twisted logic slavery was seen as a kindness.

Slaves were despised as a class in Roman culture because manual labor was universally looked down upon. The goal of the value system of upper class Roman society was not to have a respected profession but to have no profession at all, to live a life of organized leisure. Jobs we hold in high regard today, such as doctors, lawyers and artists, were given to slaves in the first century.

Slaves were regarded with suspicion. Cato the Elder, who wrote extensively on the care and feeding of slaves, said, "He who has a slave has an enemy." To call someone a slave was regarded as a serious insult. However, ancient sources mention that it was better to be the slave of a rich man than a pauper who is owned by no one. An oft-repeated phrase was "A poor free man must yield way in the marketplace to a rich man's slave."

Even the posture of a slave was detested in the time of the New Testament. In none of the numerous cults of Roman religion is there an example of kneeling. In the temples that dotted the countryside and dominated the cities, to Diana, Zeus, Aesculapius,

Fortuna, Apollo, Augustus, Nike and any of a thousand others, no one ever kneeled since kneeling was associated with the shame of slavery. To fall on your knees, in the Roman imagination, was not a sign of worship but rather humiliation. The image of Jesus on his knees washing the disciples' feet would have been offensive to Romans. This helps us enter the world of the first-century believer who knelt at services where they would wash one another's feet and confess Jesus as Lord.

In our own time kneeling has fallen out of fashion in most evangelical churches. It is practiced primarily in liturgical congregations. As we lose the practice of kneeling for confession and prayer, we subtly move away from the image of the slave of Christ.

Roman slaves have left virtually no voice in history. All we possess are the plays of Roman writers like Plautus or Petronius, who ridicule and caricature slaves, taking every opportunity to make them look foolish and ignorant. Freed slaves ("freedmen") who aspired to act above their station in life were the particular targets of their sarcasm. The only direct records we have of slaves' words are a few inscriptions left by slaves on the tombs of their masters. They are often touching examples of a closeness that sometimes developed between masters and household slaves. There are even examples of freedman and master being buried together in the same tomb.

The hopelessness of the life of the majority of Roman slaves can hardly be imagined. Sexual abuse was common and accepted as a matter of course. Half of female slaves died before age thirty. Provision for the average slave was meager. Cato speaks of a new cloak and shoes every two years. It is significant that archeologists have never verified sleeping quarters for slaves, which leaves us to assume that they were forced to sleep wherever they could find a quiet place. Slaves were *vocale instrumentum,* "tools that speak," and nothing more.

The plight of a runaway slave in Roman times was serious. Runaway slaves could be mutilated and have their eyes put out or ears cut off. Many were put to death. Horace comments on the harshness of a master who crucified a starving slave for stealing a piece of bread. When caught the slave was completely at the mercy of his master, though later, during the reign of Claudius some protective laws were enacted. Runaway slaves could be branded on the face or forearm with the letters FUG, for *fugitivus.* (Centuries later Constantine enacted a law that forbade branding on the face, reasoning that even slaves were created in the image of God.) Often habitual runaways were fitted with iron collars.

One frequently misunderstood aspect of Roman slavery is the notion that it always provided "upward mobility," that an industrious slave could move up the ladder toward eventual freedom. This is often cited as one of the major differences between African American and Roman slavery. It has mistakenly been said that Roman slavery "was always moving toward manumission."

The truth is the *cursus honorum* (Latin for "course of honors") was completely closed to any and every slave. While it is true that many Roman household and professional slaves were manumitted or even purchased their own freedom from their own savings (from a personal fund called the *peculium*), the fact remains that the overwhelming majority of slaves, those who suffered in the fields and mines, had no hope of ever knowing freedom and died miserably in their chains. On the monument Trajan's Column in Rome there are images of men killing themselves to avoid becoming Roman slaves. They could hardly have believed that slavery was an opportunity for upward mobility! Their sole way out of the hopelessness of bondage was what ex-slave Reverend Thomas Jones referred to as the only real friend a poor slave ever had: death.

To be a slave in the mines was the worst torture. John was condemned as a slave to the marble quarries of Patmos where it was assumed he would eventually choke to death on the marble dust. To be sentenced to the mines was to be sentenced to death. It is a miracle that John somehow survived, eventually returning to pastor in Ephesus.

A supremely horrific picture comes from recent excavations of ancient Roman silver mines in Rio Tinto, Spain. Some three hundred feet below the surface a number of enormous wooden water wheels were unearthed, twelve to twenty-four feet in diameter. They were used to raise water to the surface and keep the deep vein mines from flooding. Slaves, like hamsters on a wheel, turned the devices. Imagine toiling in sweltering heat and suffocating fumes, a hundred yards beneath the sunlit surface of the earth, in pitch darkness for hours at a time, occasionally being drenched by icy water that leaked from the buckets on the wheel and knowing this was your lot for the rest of your life. This could be an image of hell—and an accurate picture of the lives of many Roman slaves.

To add to the hopelessness, slaves also lived "fatherless lives." The paternity of Roman slave children was virtually never recognized since the slave master was also the paterfamalias, the undisputed head of the family. The master, whether genetically or not, acted the role of the father. We see this same kind of paternalism in the African American slave experience. Owing to the prevalence of sexual abuse, sometimes the master of the child being sold on the auction block was also the father. Slave owners in both the Roman and American worlds would often be guilty of selling their own children.

One last observation can help us enter emotionally into the life situation of a Roman slave. Remember that the institution of slavery coexisted in the midst of an evolving legal system that zealously protected the freedoms of the few (the "citizen") while at the same time legalizing the brutalization of the slave class. This is an important piece of the puzzle if we want to begin to reimagine the utterly helpless, hopeless condition of a slave in the New Testament world. A slave, who had absolutely no rights, performed his or her menial, often humiliating tasks in the presence of men and women who reveled in a measure of freedom that had been hitherto unknown before the Roman Empire. Absolute, demeaning submission lived out alongside total freedom. This was the life situation of most of the slaves we meet in the New Testament, the slaves to whom Paul addressed his advice in the household codes of Ephesians and Colossians, the slaves who were among the first believers in the Gentile world.

AFRICAN AMERICAN SLAVERY

African American slavery provides a vital lens through which we can understand the slavery of New Testament times. African and Roman slavery share far more similarities than differences. The voices from slave narratives speak of an experience that was often virtually indistinguishable from a first century slave.

As in Roman times, slaveholders in America had a paranoid preoccupation with runaway slaves. "Slave catching" was a profession, and giving aid to a runaway was a serious and punishable offense. As in Roman times, runaway slaves, if they were not executed as an example to others, were collared and branded.

As in Roman times, slaves were poorly provided for. Frederick Douglass remembered that most slave children went naked and were forced to eat boiled corn meal from a trough on the ground. Both Douglass and Thomas Jones commented that slaves were provided with only two shirts, one pair of pants and one jacket per year.

As in Roman times, there was a vast difference between the life of a "house slave" and a "field hand." Douglass again speaks of regularly seeing men beaten to death in the fields, where there were often no witnesses, while household slaves lived in relative comfort, yet were still subject to the whim of the master or mistress.

As in Roman times, American slavery existed in a political context where our founding fathers put forth the notion that "all men are created equal," and that freedom was an "inalienable right." In fact, the founders' greatest complaint against King George was that he was enslaving them. Like first-century slaves, African American slaves were forced to exist within the context of this galling discrepancy where the same Constitution that granted whites freedom determined, in Article One, that they were to be valued (taxed) as only three-fifths of a person. Men and women were made slaves on the basis of what ex-slave Lunsford Lane referred to as "the crime of wearing colored skin."

Emotionally, spiritually, physically, relationally, the American slave experience was fundamentally the same as Roman slaves of the first century. They were owned by another person who exercised total control over their bodies, their lives and the lives of their children. They had virtually no rights that a free person was bound to recognize. Their life situation fragmented and destroyed families. The similarities between the two worlds far outweigh the differences. They represent, therefore, a valuable resource if we want to understand biblical slavery at the level of the imagination.

There is one important difference between the worlds of Roman and American slavery. Except for those few tomb inscriptions, we have not a single word preserved from any slave from the Roman period. We do however possess a vast record of the voices of African American slaves. We have the articulate writings of Frederick Douglass, Booker T. Washington, Mary Prince, Moses Roper, Lunsford Lane, Moses Grandy and Olaudah Equiano. We have the elegant poetry of Phyllis Wheatley and Paul Laurence Dunbar. We can still listen to the haunting laments known as "Negro spirituals," the songs of the slaves as they labored and longed for freedom.

Both the first-century church and the African American church had deep roots in slavery. Given the similarities, African American slaves can potentially speak (and even sing) for their voiceless first-century brothers and sisters. If we wish to engage Scripture we cannot disregard these eloquent voices.

PART TWO

BECOMING SLAVES OF CHRIST

4

I, Paul, a Slave of Christ

ONCE UPON A TIME A POWERFUL religious leader was traveling the Damascus road, north from Jerusalem, a journey of 175
backbreaking miles. He was on a mission, determined, unstoppa-
ble, focused, filled with self-righteous anger. Like so many others,
he was willing to kill for his religious convictions, though pre-
sumably not yet ready to die for them. He had labored a lifetime at
the meticulous observances of first-century rabbinic Judaism. In
fact, he considered himself a "Pharisee of the Pharisees." He was
in control. He had earned the privileges of his rank.

What he could only later describe as a "glittering" flash of light
knocked him from his mount. As he lay sightless on the ground he
heard for the first time a voice he would be straining to hear for
the rest of his life.

"Saul, Saul, why are you persecuting me?

"Who are you, *Master [kyrios]*?" Saul stammered.

An influential religious leader fell off his horse just outside Damascus that hot afternoon, but he came to his senses on his hands
and knees, as a slave. When Jesus appointed a frightened believer
who lived nearby named Ananias to lay his hands on Saul and heal
his blindness, he told the reluctant disciple, "I will certainly show
him how much he must suffer for my name!" (Acts 9:16). Later, on

trial before King Agrippa, Saul, whose name had been changed to Paul (slaves were usually renamed when they were purchased) would give an extended account of the rest of the message he heard on his knees that day in the middle of the road. In Acts 26:16 he confesses that Jesus had also said, "I have appointed you as a *servant* [*hyperetes,* one who serves a master or superior] and a witness."

Now that he had been struck blind he was ready to perceive the mystery of true freedom, to be freed *from* the influence and rank of the Pharisees and freed *to* take up the gentle yoke of servant-hood to Jesus. Now that he was frightened and humiliated, on his knees, he was ready to become one of the most fearless spokesmen for Christ the world has ever known. Now that he knew the identity of his Master (*kyrios*), he was ready to become his slave.

When you look at the life of Paul, when you understand the severity of his calling, you begin to see that the title "slave of Christ" is more than a metaphor. It is an accurate description of someone who gave up everything, his choices, his expectations and all his rights. Even though his Jewish background might have reckoned the term "slave of the Lord" as one of honor, remember that Paul lived in the Roman world, where being anyone's slave was seen as a mark of humiliation.

The Bible always speaks a living word into the world because it is itself alive. When Paul calls himself a "slave" to Christ he is speaking a newly born word. "I *slaved* for the Master with *lowliness of mind* [*tapeinophrosyne*] and tears," he tells the Ephesians as he bids them farewell after three years serving them (Acts 20:19, author's translation). The word translated "lowliness of mind" or sometimes "humility" is a Greek word associated with slavery in the ancient writings of Plato and Plutarch. It provides a picture of the humble slave who, in simplicity, goes about his daily chores.

Later both Paul and his close companion Peter would encourage believers using this very same word, urging them to, "clothe yourselves with *humility*" (1 Peter 3:12; cf. Colossians 3:12). Paul describes himself as "less than the least" (Ephesians 3:8). And he says, "I became a *slave [diakonos]* of this gospel by the gift of God's grace" (Ephesians 3:7; see also 1 Thessalonians 2:9).

SLAVERY TO JESUS: A GIFT OF GRACE?

Slavery echoes again and again in the world of Paul's words. It is an image he holds onto as if it were a precious gift, which of course, it is. In Paul's thought, gifts of grace flow from slavery. Worlds come together in his words as he works out the intricate connections between the freedom of being Christ's slaves and the slavery of remaining unredeemed in the world.

The fundamental links in his mind between slavery and the gifts of Christ are revealed most forcibly in his vocabulary. The words Paul chooses to describe three of the greatest gifts of grace, justification, redemption and reconciliation, come to us from the world of slavery, which for Paul had become a world of grace.

JUSTIFICATION

In one of the most frequently quoted passages on the gifts of grace, Romans 3:23-24, Paul writes, "for all have sinned and fall short of the glory of God and are *justified* freely by his grace" (NIV). The word he uses here, *dikaioo*, refers to a "judicial acquittal," of doing justice toward another person, to vindicate them, placing them once more in right relationship. In the context of slavery the word spoke of the master bestowing liberty to a slave upon manumission (literally "letting go of the hand"). In Paul's mind, to become justified meant to be restored to right relationship due to the fact that someone else, his Master, had fully vindicated and set him free.

In the first century, even after a slave had been set free, he still maintained an interdependent relationship with his master. Just because you had become a "freedman," it did not necessarily follow that you were free. In fact, the ongoing relationship between master and freedman often led to a deeper relationship. Tomb inscriptions from the New Testament period reveal that freedmen were often buried with their masters, or that their tombs had been paid for by their masters. Once our Master justifies us, a deepening of our relationship with him occurs. Discipleship inevitably follows and flows out of justification.

> For he who is called by the Lord as a slave is the Lord's freedman. (1 Corinthians 7:22)

REDEMPTION

Paul uses two different words that are translated into English as "redemption." The first, *apolytrosis*, refers to the process of buying back a slave, of paying the ransom to set one free (Romans 3:24; 8:23; 1 Corinthians 1:30; Ephesians 1:7, 14; 4:30; Colossians 1:14; compare with Luke 2:38; Hebrews 9:12). This word is based on the Greek verb *lyo*, which refers to freeing someone from prison. As a noun (*lytron*) it is usually translated "ransom."

While this is the word he uses most frequently for "redemption," one other vivid term Paul makes use of is *exagorazo* (Galatians 4:5), which literally means "to purchase out of the agora or marketplace." The simpler form *agorazo*, means "to buy." To be redeemed, in Paul's imagination, means to be bought back, as a slave is purchased from the slave market (1 Corinthians 6:20; 7:23). Paul makes it clear however that the price paid was not a purse full of silver coins, but the blood of Jesus. He is the Master who becomes the slave to purchase his servants with his own life.

RECONCILIATION

The third gift of grace Paul speaks of through the language of slavery is reconciliation (Romans 5:11; 11:15; 2 Corinthians 5:18). The word he uses *(katallage)* carries with it the image of reuniting two people who have been estranged. The word is derived from the root *allasso,* which simply means "to alter or change." In the context of slavery, the word paints a picture of a slave whose position in life has been unalterably changed. Once separated from his rights, he has become free once more.

Ransomed from the slave market, graciously invited into a new relationship of intimacy with his Master, unalterably changed by the gift of freedom—these are the slave images that come to life in the world of Paul's language. He abruptly transitioned from a lifestyle in which he may very well have owned slaves (well-known rabbis of Paul's day, like Gamaliel, possessed slaves) to a way of life built from a blueprint provided by first-century slavery. His conversion experience on the road to Damascus set Paul's life on the same trajectory as his Master Jesus. He would live that life out to the full—experientially, emotionally and theologically.

On his hands and knees he had cried out, "Who are you, Master?" In the long course of his servitude he would learn the answer to that question: his Master was a slave as well. He had purchased his servant Paul out of the agora of the world at the unimaginable cost of his own life. The world had offered Paul power and position that promised freedom but delivered slavery in the end. Jesus called him to become a slave and thereby discover a better freedom.

5

My Son, Onesimus

**For perhaps this is why he was separated [from you] for
a brief time, so that you might get him back permanently,
no longer as a slave, but more than a slave—as a dearly
loved brother.**

PHILEMON 15-16

WHENEVER YOU LISTEN TO PAUL SPEAK about slavery, imagine a solitary man standing just behind him in the shadows. He stands erect, not with the stoop-shouldered posture of a slave. He looks us straight in the eye with a compassionate countenance. His name is Onesimus. If you are to reimagine the word *slavery* as Paul uses it, you must always imagine him lingering there.

When he ran away from his master, Philemon, Onesimus wasn't simply fleeing from one man to another, but from one world to another. In the Jewish world of Paul, the Torah dictated that runaway slaves were to be sheltered (Exodus 21:21; Deuteronomy 23:15-16). In Philemon's world, Roman law decreed that runaways would be severely punished, along with the person who offered them shelter. The African American slave would have been in an identical situation. But in Paul's time there was no underground railroad for someone like Onesimus. He would have been completely on his own.

We have examples from the ancient world of other "letters of appeal" for runaway slaves. One instance comes to us from Pliny the Younger, nephew and adopted son of Pliny the Elder, a respected writer of natural history and close friend of the Emperor Vespasian. Pliny the Younger was well known for his benevolent character. In the following letter to his friend Sabinianus, Pliny makes an appeal on the behalf of a runaway freedman. Notice that even though he is no longer technically a slave, a binding relationship still exists between the two men. Unlike Paul's letter to Philemon, Pliny is appealing to the slave owner on the basis of the depth of the repentance of the runaway. Paul's appeal is founded on the mutual relationship they all have in Christ.

To Sabinianus

Your freedman, whom you lately mentioned to me with displeasure, has been with me, and threw himself at my feet with as much submission as he could have fallen at yours. He earnestly requested me with many tears, and even with all the eloquence of silent sorrow, to intercede for him; in short, he convinced me by his whole behaviour that he sincerely repents of his fault. I am persuaded he is thoroughly reformed, because he seems deeply sensible of his guilt. I know you are angry with him, and I know, too, it is not without reason; but clemency can never exert itself more laudably than when there is the most cause for resentment. You once had an affection for this man, and, I hope, will have again; meanwhile, let me only prevail with you to pardon him. If he should incur your displeasure hereafter, you will have so much the stronger plea in excuse for your anger as you shew yourself more merciful to him now. Concede something to his youth, to his tears, and to your own natural mildness of temper: do not make him uneasy any longer, and I will add, too, do not make yourself so; for a man of your kindness of heart cannot be angry without feeling great uneasiness. I am afraid, were I to join my entreaties with his, I should seem rather to compel than request you to forgive him. Yet I will not scruple even to write mine with his; and in so much the stronger terms as I have very sharply and severely reproved him, positively threatening never to interpose again in his behalf. But though it was proper to say this to him, in order to make him more fearful of offending, I do not say so to you. I may perhaps, again have occasion to entreat you upon his account, and again obtain your forgiveness; supposing, I mean, his fault should be such as may become me to intercede for, and you to pardon. Farewell.

When he was on the road speaking for the abolition of slavery, Frederick Douglass would introduce himself by saying, "Do you see this head? Do you see these hands? I stole them from my master." During the time of slavery in America, as in the time of Onesimus, a runaway slave was considered to be a thief who had literally stolen himself from his master. If caught he was liable for the wages he would have earned during the time lost as well as the price that had been paid for his own bondage. In Douglass's time a runaway could flee north toward freedom. In the first century there was virtually nowhere to run.

In April of 1851, a very different letter of appeal was written on behalf of a runaway slave named Thomas X. Sims. The letter was addressed to a black congregation that met in an abandoned theater. (Paul's letter to Philemon was also addressed to a congregation.) The letter is a request for their prayers. Eventually Sims was returned to his owner, James Potter of Savannah. He was later sold into Tennessee.

Dear Friend,

The innocent man, now in chains in the Boston Court House, has under his own hand, requested to be remembered in our prayers. I am sure that the men and women, who assemble at the Melodeon this morning, do not need this formal request to remind them, of the terrible and threatening evils, which hang over this man. They will pray most fervently, that he may escape from the horrible pit that yawns beneath his feet. Their prayers will not be an empty formality, but will go out with one accord, with brotherly affection, from sincere and devout hearts.

Please read to the congregation, Mr. Sims own request, it may be the last words he will ever address to us: which are as follows:

"The undersigned, a free man, and in peril, desires the prayers of this congregation that God may deliver him from the oppressor, and restore him to freedom."

Boston April 5 1851
Thomas X. Sims

We can piece together the life situation of the letter called Philemon by reading between the lines. Philemon, Onesimus's master, was a member of the house church in Colossae. Onesimus and Tychicus (who may have also been a slave) are mentioned in Colossians 4:7-9 as bearers of the letter to the church there. The leader of the church, named Archippus, was a companion of Paul.

Along with the letter we have come to know as Colossians, the two were also delivering the letter of appeal to Onesimus's master, Philemon, a letter which is also meant to be read before "the church that meets in your house."

Onesimus was one of the three most common slave names of the first century. (The other two were Eros and Hermes.) Upon purchasing a slave the owner customarily gave them a new name that reflected the identity of their bondage. Each time a person was sold they might take on a new name and thereby lose a part of their identity. (The process was virtually identical in African American slavery.) One popular name given to slaves by their masters was Philodespotes, meaning "master lover."

The name Philemon gave to his slave Onesimus means "useful." Paul, perhaps poking fun at the pompous custom, writes in verse 11, "Once he was *useless* to you, but now he is *useful* both to you and to me." Ironically, as a result of his running away, Onesimus had undergone a transformation. He had grown into his name. He who once was a useless, desperate runaway had become useful to the cause of the gospel.

He sought out Paul in Rome because of some previous contact with him in Colossae, where he had been a slave in the household of Philemon. In the interim while serving Paul, who was under house arrest in Rome (though some scholars believe Paul might have still been in Ephesus), Onesimus had come to faith in Jesus. The runaway slave had fled almost a thousand miles from Colossae to where Paul was imprisoned in Rome. This was at a time when the average traveler could hope to cover only fifteen to twenty miles a day on foot.

The slave owner, Philemon, had been introduced to Christ through Paul's ministry, a fact that Paul deliberately uses in his appeal for Onesimus (vv. 8, 19). Before he can secure his forgiveness, Paul must help Philemon to see his slave no longer as a piece of his property, but now as a person. Paul includes what we would call an IOU. In verses 18-19 he makes a legally binding promise to repay any debt Onesimus might owe his master, whether as a result of running away or to repay any money he might have stolen to provide for his flight.

In excavations all around the Mediterranean, archaeologists have unearthed circular metal bands that usually contain as a part of the inscription the words "Capture me, for I am fleeing." For a time scholars wondered if these were only ancient dog collars. But owing to their large size and the fact that many contained longer inscriptions that indicated otherwise, most academics have now concluded that these are, in fact, slave collars. Some wore the humiliating "fugitive" collars, like animals, for the rest of their lives.

There is no indication as to weather Onesimus was wearing a slave collar inscribed "Capture me, for I am fleeing" when he found Paul. But certainly he was fleeing, though he never expected that he would be captured by Christ and in time become his slave. There is no word as to the reception he received upon his return to Philemon. We are left with the expectation that Philemon and the church of Colossae welcomed the runaway just as Paul had asked.

Beyond any play on words based on the slave's name, Paul's most significant statement, discreetly tucked into the body of the letter, comes in verse 10: "I appeal to you for *my son* Onesimus" (NIV, my emphasis). He has not simply sheltered the young man, nor merely preached the gospel to him; Paul has taken Onesimus, the slave, into his very heart (v. 12). He has adopted him into his faith family. How then should Philemon receive the runaway Onesimus? Why, as Paul's son, of course. Philemon had named him "useful." Paul had given him a new name he had never known, "my son."

Of all the subtle hints contained in the letter, verse 17 is perhaps one of the most subtle and meaningful, and yet we usually read right past it. "Welcome him as you would welcome me," Paul writes (NIV). When Jesus sent out his disciples he granted them a remarkable yet concealed dignity:

> If the world hates you, understand that it hated Me before it hated you. If you were of the world, the world would love [you as] its own. However, because you are not of the world, but I have chosen you out of it, the world hates you. Remember the word I spoke to you: "A *slave* is not greater than his *master.*" If they persecuted Me, they will also persecute you. If they kept My word, they will also keep yours. (John 15:18-20, my emphasis)

Jesus was in effect giving his authority to his apostles, his "sent ones." In verse 17 Paul is quietly doing the same thing for Onesimus. When he appears at the door of Philemon's home the way he is received should resemble the way Paul would be welcomed. The place of leadership Onesimus eventually attained in the church at Ephesus is a hint at how he was received back by Philemon and the church that met in his house.

As he brings his brief letter to a close, Paul tells Philemon he is certain that his friend will do even more than he has asked, that he will exceed his expectations of forgiving Onesimus and restoring him to a place in his family (v. 21). And then, "just one more thing," Paul writes. "Prepare your guest room for me." That is, Paul could show up at any time to see if Philemon had honored his requests concerning the slave, Onesimus.

Paul closes with greetings from the brothers who are his fellow prisoners. There is their familiar friend, Epaphras, who was also from Colossae. In Colossians 4:12 he is described as "Epaphras, who is one of you, *a slave of Christ Jesus*, greets you. He is always contending [wrestling] for you in his prayers." Keep in mind that wrestlers in the arena were always slaves, so both the images Paul uses to describe Epaphras's work for the believers in Colossae call to mind the image of the faithful slave. In fact, in the same breath, Paul calls Epaphras a slave (*doulos*) of Christ. Mark is there as well, having been reconciled to Paul after the dispute which involved Barnabas (Acts 15:37-40).

Aristarchus, who seemed to be everywhere with Paul, sends his greetings as well. And finally there are Demas and Luke, both former slaves, their names exhibiting shortened forms, nicknames known as "hypocorisms." This was another method for naming slaves in the first century. For example, a man named Lucius would give his slave a form of his own name, hence the name "Loukas," which we translate as "Luke." Demas could also be such a slave nickname derived from a shortened form of the name "Demetrius." Their names always appear together, and it is suspicious that Paul never refers to either of them as "slaves." Instead he grants them the title "fellow workers," a designation that had nothing to do with slavery. It is a title he also uses for Philemon (v. 1)! It appears that Paul refers to free men, like himself, as slaves. To slaves who are laboring alongside him, he gives the name "fellow workers."

Why was such a brief, seemingly insignificant letter preserved and accepted into the canon of Scripture by the church fathers? We have seen that when Ignatius was traveling to Rome where he would be martyred for his faith in Christ, he was met by various delegations from local churches. Just outside Smyrna, he met the bishop of the local congregation, Polycarp. One of the other men had come from the church at Ephesus. He was the bishop there. His name was Onesimus. The presence of the letter in the canon and the name of the bishop of Ephesus are beyond coincidence. The runaway slave had become the successor to John himself, the leader of one of the greatest churches in the early Christian world. His story offers hope for all of us who are running away.

WHY WASN'T PAUL AN ABOLITIONIST?

As we read Paul's thoughts in regard to slaves and slavery the inevitable question arises: "Why wasn't Paul a William Wilberforce?" In the letter to Philemon there is no tone of judgment from Paul against the institution of slavery. There is no moral indignation. Paul is not writing, indeed never writes, to abolish slavery.

During the time of slavery in America this apparent absence of outrage was twisted by slave owners into a "biblical" justification that was preached from pulpits in the North as well as the South. Though it is rarely recognized, it is a miracle in itself that so many African slaves came to Christ amid this heretical climate, that so many found the true gospel of Jesus despite their chains. It is a historical wonder that so many of those marginalized and abused, before they even learned to read, had a superior understanding of the grace of the One to whom they prayed as "Master." Surely the reason so many of their hearts resonated with the heart of Jesus is because they recognized in him the life and calling of a slave.

There is no Jew or Greek, slave or free, male or female; for you are all one in Christ Jesus. (Galatians 3:28)

Every time Paul proclaimed the oneness every follower of Jesus
has with one another, he was, in a sense, pronouncing slavery
"null and void." In the light of Christ it simply did not exist any-
more. But this spiritual reality was not at all evident to the pagan
world in which the new Christians were living out this new freedom. Paul did not directly confront the world of Roman slavery
because his call was to introduce another world shaped by a tran-
scendent value system derived from the servant life of Jesus. He
did not preach the end of slavery, but rather a new kind of slavery
that was a new beginning, a better freedom.

6

Eye-Slaves
and People-Pleasers

Slaves, obey your human masters [*kyriois*] in everything; don't work only while being watched [*ophthalmodoulia*], in order to please men [*anthropareskoi*], but [work] wholeheartedly, fearing the Lord [*kyrios*]. Whatever you do, do it enthusiastically, as something done for the Lord [*kyrios*] and not for men, knowing that you will receive the reward of an inheritance from the Lord [*kyrios*]—you serve the Lord [*kyrios*] Christ. For the wrongdoer will be paid back for whatever wrong he has done, and there is no favoritism. Masters [*kyrioi*], supply your slaves with what is right and fair, since you know that you too have a Master [*kyrios*] in heaven.

COLOSSIANS 3:22–4:1

POET, BELIEVER AND FORMER SLAVE Lunsford Lane described his experience attending a white Episcopal church where the "kindhearted" minister concluded each sermon by reminding the slaves, "It is the will of heaven from all eternity that we be slaves, and our masters be our owners." Lane concluded that eventually most of us left him, for like some of the faint-hearted disciples in early times we said, "This is a hard saying, who can bear it?" I often heard select portions of the scriptures read. And on the Sabbath there was one sermon preached expressly for the colored people, which it was generally my privilege to hear. I became familiar with the texts, "Servants be obedient to your masters." "Not with eye service as men pleasers." "He that knoweth his master's will and doeth it not, shall be beaten with many stripes." . . . They formed the basis of most of the public instructions to us. The first commandment impressed upon our minds was to obey your masters and the second was like unto it, namely, to do as much work when they or the overseers were not watching us as when they were.

Two parallel passages, one from Colossians and the other from Ephesians (Ephesians 5:22–6:9), provide a precious window into the world of the first-century Christian slave. We will focus on the passage from Colossians since it is directly connected with Philemon, who was part of a house church in Colossae (Colossians 4:7-9). It is interesting to imagine the owner of the runaway slave, Philemon, sitting with his congregation hearing these words about slaves, addressed to him as well as his entire community of faith.

These two passages are referred to as the "household codes," for in them Paul offers advice to every member of the house—to fathers, mothers, children and finally to slaves.

In his advice to slaves Paul uses two fascinating compound words drawn from the vocabulary of slavery; *ophthalmodoulia* and *anthropareskoi*. Both expressions reach out and grab our imaginations. The first word requires an entire sentence to translate. *Oph-*

thalmodoulia is a combination of the word *ophthalmos* or "eye" (we get our word "ophthalmologist" from this root) and the basic word for "slave," which is *doulos*. Literally the word means "eye-slavery." "Be obedient," says Paul, "don't be eye-slaves, that is, only slaving away when someone's eye is upon you" (see Matthew 6:1; Luke 22:25).

The next combination word, which is more familiar to us, provides a parallel or synonym to *ophthalmodoulia*. It is the word *anthropareskoi*. It brings together the word for "man," *anthropos,* with the word *aresko*, "to please." It is translated "people-pleasers." The word does not represent a relationship but rather a frame of mind. It was used in antiquity to refer to those who had deliberately made the decision to please people rather than God. Plato said, "A man should not try to please his fellow slaves but his good and noble masters."

Together the two words paint a picture in the imagination of the slave who only worked when someone was taking notice, who only performed his duties when he knew he would receive commendation from his master. They illustrate how profoundly Paul's understanding of the gospel was shaped by the world and vocabulary of slavery.

Paul encourages slaves in Christian households to avoid the temptation of falling into this frame of mind. When they are at work, whether anyone is watching or not, they should work with a "sincere heart" and with "all enthusiasm," literally to work "from your soul." Verse 23 contains the true motivation. They should work as to the *Kyrios,* as to the Lord and true Master, Jesus.

This passage has a subtle nuance that is not reflected in most English translations. There is an interplay between the singular *kyrios* and its plural form *kyrioi.* The shifting from one to the other creates a tension that, I believe, Paul deliberately intends. When referring to the slave owners (kyrios) most translations opt for the word "masters" or perhaps "owners." (One of the original definitions for the word kyrios was "one who owns possessions.") But when the singular form of the same word appears (kyrios) most translations use "Lord." When the passage is translated this way the tension that Paul intended is lost. The purpose of the slave section of the household code is to make the point that both groups, owners as well as those who are owned, have one Kyrios, one Owner, one Lord. They are, none of them, to be "eye-slaves" or "people-pleasers."

This is driven home in the final section of the household code, found in the first verse of chapter four. It is a word addressed to the slave owners, the kyrioi. "Owners," says Paul, "treat your slaves with justice and fairness, knowing that you also have an Owner (kyrios) in heaven."

Paul reminds the slaves that they should be faithful because they have a Master who will reward them in due time (Colossians 3:24). Likewise he warns the slave owners that they also are owned by Someone in heaven, to whom they are accountable.

Paul's purpose is not abolition, but rather an inner, spiritual, transformation that must occur in both the slaves and their owners. The motivation must be love; obedience and respect from one group and compassion and justice from the other. None of it would be possible were it not for the lordship of Jesus Christ over all of them. They are, all of them, owned. And this ownership must mean everything or it does not mean anything. Every other distinction disappears by comparison (Galatians 3:28).

In a similar passage, writing to Timothy, Paul says:

All who are under the yoke as slaves must regard their own masters to be worthy of all respect, so that God's name and His teaching will not be blasphemed. And those who have believing masters should not be disrespectful to them because they are brothers, but should serve them better, since those who benefit from their service are believers and dearly loved. (1 Timothy 6:1-2)

Biblical obedience is always rooted in love, the obedience that endures humiliation and mistreatment. Saying "Your will be done" is really constantly expressing "I love you." This is the obedience that Paul encourages from both the owner and the owned. He is not calling for a reshuffling of power but rather a rearrangement of our core values in accordance with the image of faithful slave.

7

Your Father's Name

And because you are sons, God has sent the Spirit of His Son into our hearts, crying, "Abba, Father!" So you are no longer a slave, but a son; and if a son, then an heir through God.

GALATIANS 4:6-7

I WAS WRITING A NOTE TO MY OLDEST DAUGHTER the day she left home for college. When I signed it I looked down at what I'd written: "Dad." To everyone who knows me, to my wife, to my friends, I am known simply as "Mike." But only to my children am I "Dad." It is a unique title for a unique relationship. No one else but my children can ever call me by that name.

During the time of slavery in America, there were two things virtually every slave could not tell you—his birthday or the name of his father. Since the institution of slavery destroyed the families of the slaves, paternity was almost never recorded, nor was the day a slave was born. (A few exceptions were recorded in family Bibles.)

Frederick Douglass, whose last name was originally "Bailey" from his former owner, describes in his autobiography the process of eventually deciding for himself what his name would be, the name which would eventually become so famous. Booker T. Washington chose his own last name when he noticed that the other children had two names while he only had one.

In Romans 8:15 Paul describes the process of our spiritual liberation. He writes, "For you did not receive a spirit of slavery to fall back into fear, but you received the Spirit of adoption, by whom we cry out, 'Abba, Father!'" Paul lays before us the promise that the deliverance Jesus Christ offers includes with it a new level of intimacy with God. He says that the spirit of adoption, which we receive when we accept Christ as our Master, enables us to know God by a unique new name, "Abba." One of the closest translations of the Hebrew word is "Dad."

As the adopted children of God, as heirs of God and fellow heirs with Jesus, we can look at our long lost spiritual birth certificate and read there on the line that indicates paternity; "Abba, Father." Though the world sought to rob us of this precious knowledge, the Spirit tells us the name of our Father.

BOUGHT AT A PRICE

Hanging on the wall of my study is a simple, worn wooden chair. If you were to see it in a yard sale it probably wouldn't occur to you to make a bid on it. But it is very valuable to me.

It was made around 1816, by a man named Dick Poyner, a slave who lived just two miles from where I live today. It is especially precious because with the extra money he made building these simple chairs Dick purchased his freedom around 1850, and later that of his wife, Millie. It was extremely rare, especially in the South, for a slave to find the means to buy themselves out of slavery. There are examples of local churches paying a part of the fee to liberate a slave who then became their pastor.

In the world of the New Testament it was also possible and a bit more common for a slave to purchase his or her own freedom. Household slaves were allowed to accumulate a *peculium*, a fund that could be used for their own manumission, though they sometimes used the money to buy their own slaves! Still we must remember that in the first century, as in American slavery, for the vast majority of slaves there was no way out. They would die in their chains.

In 1 Corinthians 6:20, Paul reminds his readers that they are not their own; they have been bought at a price. He repeats the statement in the next chapter (7:23). He writes to a community where up to half of the population would have been owned by someone else. In a wealthy city like Corinth personal slaves would have been numerous, as well as cultic prostitutes who were often slaves donated by their owners to "serve" in the temple.

Paul, who often signs himself "a slave to Christ" (Romans 1:1; Titus 1:1; Ephesians 3:7), wants his readers in Corinth to know while it might have been possible for some slaves to earn enough money to buy their freedom, they could never truly pay the price for themselves. Only the price paid on the cross of Christ can purchase their freedom and ours, reconciling us to God. Paul uses the slave word "reconcile" (Romans 5:10; 2 Corinthians 5:18, 20), the "bringing together of those who had been separated from each other."

We belong to the One who, in effect, bought us. The New Testament does not offer the choice between slavery and freedom, but only whose slave we will be—the world's or Christ's. Jesus does not offer freedom from slavery but instead a new kind of slavery that provides the only true freedom. I cannot buy my freedom. Only Jesus can.

8

Don't Worry About It

Each person should remain in the life situation in which he was called. Were you called while a slave? It should not be a concern to you.

1 CORINTHIANS 7:20-21

PAUL'S FINAL WORD TO SLAVES in 1 Corinthians is the most scandalous. To men and women living in bondage he literally says, "Don't have a care," or perhaps "Don't worry about it." Shouldn't these words anger and frustrate us? How much more insensitive and politically incorrect could Paul possibly be? How could these words possibly resonate with the branded or collared slave who had come to faith in Christ? If we listen superficially we will always end up in such cul-de-sacs. But when we engage the text at the level of the imagination, reading with the heart as well as the mind, we sense the doors of the complicated world of slavery beginning to open.

It is difficult to enter the confusing, first-century world of Paul, where a freedman was still not a free man, where wealthy slaves owned their own slaves, where often it was better to become the property of a rich man than to be free but poor. Still, in many ways his world is no less confusing than our own, where the wealthy become slaves to their own lifestyles, where the freedom the world seductively offers is really slavery.

In the early church, Christians had begun to go into the slave markets and sell themselves into slavery, using the money to purchase the freedom of those who were slaves. The author of the *Apostolic Constitutions* wrote, "For a believer ought not to go to any of those public meetings, unless to purchase a slave, and save a soul."

Becoming slaves in order to set others free. It was a confusing and upside-down world, because Jesus had turned it upside down. His coming had introduced a radical reversal of identities. Those who were rich were giving everything away, becoming poor so that they might be truly rich. Those who were intellectually gifted, like Paul himself, were embracing the foolishness of the gospel in order to be truly wise. In 1 Corinthians 9:19 Paul expresses this notion when he writes, "For although I am free from all people, I have made myself a slave to all people, in order to win more people." Note Paul's movement from freedom to slavery. (See also Romans 6:22.)

When he was speaking to those who were still slaves in the church of Corinth, to those who apparently had not yet been freed by their masters, or for whom no one was willing to sell themselves to buy their freedom, Paul gives this piece of advice, which at first seems irritatingly shallow and simple minded—"Don't worry about it."

"Don't worry about it?" You can feel the animosity of some of the Corinthian slaves. "That's easy for you to say; no one owns you!"

But they would be wrong to say that. And we would be wrong to think his advice shallow. "Don't worry about it" is much the same as Jesus' often-repeated phrase "Fear not." Jesus invariably spoke those words after he had revealed a new dimension of his divinity. Paul was experiencing this in his own life, in his own personal incarnation of Jesus' life in him. He had spent his freedom to become a slave so they could be truly set free, even if they still remained slaves in this world. He had offered his freedom for theirs. Were they still in bondage to another person? There is nothing to worry about, since it is Jesus who truly is their owner.

Like the slaves in the American South who prayed loudly to Jesus as their Master to let their earthly masters know who was truly their Lord, Paul reminds the slaves in Corinth that they are now owned by the only Master whose bondage is the only freedom. If this is true, then there is nothing to worry about.

Though Paul will conclude offhandedly, "But if you can become free, by all means take the opportunity," a freedom purchased with money is not what he hopes for. Only the better freedom, purchased by the ransom of the cross of Christ, will suffice. In Paul's mind, no one can really pay for their own freedom.

9

Freed From and Freed To

WHEN WE ARE FREED FROM OUR OLD SLAVERY to the world and bound over as slaves to Christ, an exchange occurs. As we are liberated from all those things that enslaved us, we discover a new, better freedom that takes their place. When we are freed *from* the tyranny of self we discover a new freedom *to* enter redemptively into the lives of others. When we are set free from the bondage of the fear of death through the letting go of our lives, we experience a new freedom to live fully and fearlessly for our new Master. The moment Jesus sets us "free from," he also makes us "free to."

No one explores this transformation more completely than Paul, because he had himself been set free from slavery to sin, discovering in the process that he had become free to live as a slave to righteousness (Romans 7:21-25; Galatians 3:23).

You have been set free from sin and have become slaves to righteousness. (Romans 6:18 NIV)

Part of what Frederick Douglass referred to as the "gross fraud" of slavery was the use of freedom against the slaves. This was particularly true of holidays when slave owners actually encouraged heavy drinking. Later, as the slaves were suffering the effects of what we benignly refer to as a "hangover" but what is more accurately called "alcohol poisoning," Douglass says they were encour-

aged to believe "this is what freedom is like." He concluded that
the slave owners were trying to "disgust their slaves with freedom." Some decided afterward that they would rather be slaves to
their masters than slaves to rum. These unfortunate slaves had
come to understand what Peter says, "You are a slave to whatever
controls you" (2 Peter 2:19 NLT).

In Romans 6:16, Paul clearly sets forth the only choices we have
based on the premise that we are slaves to whatever or whoever
owns us. The choice for Paul is not between slavery and freedom,
but rather, whose slave will you be? The world's or Christ's? If you
have been set free *from* sin by the atoning sacrifice of Jesus then
you have been freed *to* become a slave to righteousness. "Slaves of
righteousness" is simply another title for "disciples." There is no
other choice for the disciple but to take up the cross. There is no
other choice but total submission to his lordship, his mastery, over
every area of our lives. Being a disciple, being a slave, means giving up choices.

FREED TO PLEASE OUR MASTER

> For am I now trying to win the favor of people, or God? Or
> am I striving to please people? If I were still trying to please
> people, I would not be a slave of Christ. (Galatians 1:10)

Paul seems to be talking to himself as much as the believers in
Galatia in this verse. A faction within the church had called into
question Paul's authority as an apostle and servant of Jesus. He
spends fully 40 percent of the letter defending himself from their
attacks. (See Galatians 1:1, 15-20; 2:6-9.)

A group we know as the Judiazers had infiltrated the church,
falsely teaching Gentile converts that they must become Jews be-

fore they could become proper Christians. In no other letter do we
see such a range of negative emotions in Paul. Of all his letters this
is the only one that leaves out the thanksgiving section at the beginning. Clearly there is an influential faction in the church that
does not approve of Paul or his message of grace, and the thank-
fulness had gone right out of him.

Beyond the emotionality of his letter lies a crystal-clear certainty
in Paul's heart and mind. By it he possesses a disturbing clarity of
purpose. The liberating truth is that he does not exist to win their
approval. While he longs to serve them, his ultimate purpose is not
to please them. This clarity comes from the simple fact that Paul
knows he is a slave. Someone has bought and paid for him. He is
owned. He has only one Master; only one Person to please.

This may be one of the greatest liberating realities of being a
slave to Christ. We have only him to please, we have only his approval to gain. We are never called to be people-pleasers, only
Christ-pleasers.

FREED TO HEAL DIVISIONS

Who are you to criticize another's household slave [oiketes]?
Before his own Lord he stands or falls. And stand he will!
For the Lord is able to make him stand. (Romans 14:4)

When Paul writes to the Romans, he is communicating with a
group of believers he has never met. He had avoided ministering
in Rome since the church had already been planted there, as early
as A.D. 35 (Romans 1:8-13; 15:23). When Paul first came to Rome
in A.D. 59, the church was well established. He writes the letter we
know as Romans to prepare the church for his upcoming stopover
visit on his way to Spain (Iberia).

The church had been divided in A.D. 49 when the Emperor Claudius had expelled all the Jews from Rome, due to a riot caused by someone Suetonius mistakenly identifies by the slave name "Chrestus." The name means "Good One." It was in fact a riot caused by the factions arguing about *Christos,* or Christ. It is an interesting detail that when a pagan historian confuses the title of Jesus Christ, he mistakenly gives him a slave's name.

In A.D. 50 Paul will meet two of these banished Jews, Priscilla and Aquila (Acts 18:1-2; Romans 16:3). When Claudius dies in A.D. 54 the ban is lifted and the Jews return to the city. The impact of the expulsion of the Jews on the church is that leadership, which had previously been a mixture of both Jewish and Gentile, has been dominated by the Gentiles for a period of five years. When the Jews return to Rome and to the church, there is unavoidable tension between the two groups. Paul writes to help ease the tension.

In Acts 14:4 he adopts the familiar image of the household slave (*oiketes;* see Luke 16:13, "No *slave* can serve two masters"). Since the church was known as both the "house of God" (*oikos tou theou*) as well as the "household of faith" (*oikeios tes pisteos),* the image of a household servant is one that will immediately focus the imaginations of Paul's readers.

The Gentile believers worshiped Jesus the Lord; the Jewish believers celebrated Jesus the Messiah. There were still dietary conflicts between the two groups, as well as differing styles of worship between synagogue and pagan influences. Inevitably the factions began judging each other, condemning what they did not or would not understand about the other. It is not difficult to imagine the devastating effect this would have had on the ministry of the church.

"Who are you to judge another person's slave?" Paul pleads with them. It is a matter between them and their Master. Before him and him alone will the slave stand or fall. And because of who the Master is, says Paul, he will inevitably stand. Not because of who he is, but because of who owns him. The image of standing suggests the posture of one who has been given freedom.

Now that the believers in Rome were free from judging each other they were free to get back to the business of the church; loving each other well and serving one another. The freedom from judging each other could only come from their slavery to Christ.

FREED TO SERVE

> But reject foolish and ignorant disputes, knowing that they
> breed quarrels. The Lord's slave must not quarrel, but must
> be gentle to everyone, able to teach, and patient, instructing
> his opponents with gentleness. (2 Timothy 2:23-25)

Paul had left Timothy behind in Ephesus to provide leadership to the struggling church there. There were factions causing disunity and the ever-present heresy of legalism. The second letter to Timothy is Paul's final letter. He is chained like a criminal, like a slave (2:9) in Rome. Everyone except Luke the slave had deserted him (4:11). It is believed that along with Peter, he had been caught up in the persecution under Nero that broke out against the church after the great fire in A.D. 64. It seems evident that Paul believes he will not survive past the winter (4:6-8, 21). Even with all this pressure weighing on his mind, what concerns Paul most is Timothy's ministry in Ephesus.

Knowing well the quarreling with which Timothy is having to

deal, Paul's final word to his son in the faith is centered on the image of the humble servant of Christ. Paul tells the young pastor that a "slave of the Master" (*doulon kyriou*) is free. His demeanor is dictated by his slave posture, dominated by patience and gentleness. Timothy must come to understand that whatever the struggle, it is ultimately the concern of his Master. He must focus simply and humbly on obedient service. Slaves are freed from quarreling and fighting. They are therefore free to serve through patiently teaching those who would otherwise be their opponents. It is a freedom that could only come through slavery.

As Paul writes these words to Timothy, the chains on his wrists drag across the parchment. Yet it is a decidedly free man who sends his wisdom and council to the young pastor from behind prison walls. The freedom he found on the road outside Damascus all those long years ago, every word of it has come true.

A Portrait of Slavery to Christ

If we combine the various facets of the image of the faithful slave found in Paul's writings, the picture that comes into focus is this: Slaves of Christ are those who are familiar with suffering, little food, meager clothing, no place to lay one's head at night to sleep. They exhibit "lowliness of mind," that is, true humility. They are not doormats but rather know who they are and more importantly whose they are. Their value and identity are derived completely from their Master.

They understand that a price was paid to purchase them out of the slave market. Someone recognized that they had value and was willing to pay the price. Within the context of that confidence, they obediently move through the day, steadily at work to please only their master. When others confront them, insult or abuse them, they refrain from defending themselves or quarreling with them. Even when they sense that the Master's gaze is not on what they are doing, they still work at the task with all their heart. When they see other slaves doing shabby work they do not concern themselves. That is not their concern.

With a new name and a new identity derived from the Master, they live with a new purpose and sense of direction. Even when, especially when, times are painful, they rest in the confident provision and protection of the Master.

It might seem that we jumped ahead, dealing with the Pauline passages before the Gospels. But in reality we are not moving backward, but forward now, as we look at Christ, the One who came in the image of a slave.

PART THREE

ENCOUNTERING CHRIST THE SLAVE

10

Christic the Slave

Who, being in very nature God,
did not consider equality with God
something to be grasped,
but made himself nothing,
taking the very nature of a servant *[doulos]*,
being made in human likeness.
And being found in appearance as a man,
he humbled himself
and became obedient to death—
even death on a cross!

PHILIPPIANS 2:6-8 (NIV)

As far we know, the first song the church ever sang was a song about a slave. It is a song of both servanthood and lordship. It is based on the paradox that glory comes through humiliation, that the lordship of Jesus is rooted firmly in and flows out of his slavery.

Some believe that a Roman spy, named Pliny the Younger, overheard the early Christians singing this song. (Remember, he was the person who had written the letter of appeal on behalf of the runaway freedman.) He had been sent to determine for the emperor whether the Christians posed a genuine threat to Rome. He reported back, "They gather early in the morning and sing a hymn to Christ, whom they revere as God." Scholars speculate whether that hymn was this song from Philippians 2, the "Carmen Christi" or "Hymn to Christ."

"Christ is Lord" is the earliest known confessional statement of the church. Domitian, the Roman emperor who exiled John to Patmos, tried to appropriate the title of Lord/*kyrios* for himself around A.D. 90. But the church wanted to be clear that it was not Caesar who was Lord, but Jesus.

Certainly the word *kyrios* was also understood as a title of divinity. But within its orbit, the term still affirmed absolute ownership, whether the person who bore the title was a man, or a god, or both at the same time. So that earliest of confessions, "Christ is Master," is also an affirmation that Jesus is Absolute Owner. It is the same prayer that echoed centuries later in the covert congregations of African slaves who called out to Jesus almost exclusively as "Master." They sang the echoes of their own experience:

When Israel was in Egypt's land,

Let my people go

When Harriet Tubman, the leader of the Underground Railroad and opponent of the Fugitive Slave Act, first found her freedom by escaping to Philadelphia, she saw herself as a "stranger in a strange land." She was regarded by all who knew her as a Moses figure. A century later, on the Mall in Washington, D.C., Martin Luther King Jr. would speak of racial reconciliation as the "promised land." For over 340 years of slavery, African Americans were linked to a unique understanding of the ancient creed "Jesus is Master."

Their connection to their Master Jesus was established from the very beginning, rooted in the Old Testament experience of Israel. Now Jesus was the One they were waiting on to come eventually and set them free.

Until then, he was the Suffering Servant who had entered redemptively into the excruciating experience of their slavery. "Sweet Jesus," he was often called. Perhaps the slaves loved calling him this because, even in the indescribable bitterness of their bondage, his presence also provided an indescribable sweetness. When the Master understands every stroke of the lash, every humiliating epitaph, slavery is no less painful, yet still it is redeemed. The sweetness of this knowledge inevitably led the slaves to sing to, for and about their "sweet Jesus." Their ancient Christian ancestors understood the comforting power of such songs.

In Paul's hymn in Philippians 2, the opening verse sings to us that Jesus refused to grasp equality with God (v. 6). Instead he emptied himself and assumed the "lowliness of mind" (*tapeinophrosyne*, see Ephesians 4:2) of the slave (*doulos*). Jesus portrays two qualities in the song that the believers at Philippi would have immediately associated with slaves.

First, *Jesus humbled himself.* In the *Satyricon*, Petronius writes that someone, upon arriving at a banquet, noticed a sign posted beside the door: "If any slave shall leave the house without the Master's permission, he shall receive a hundred lashes." Not a move could be made without the master's consent. Slaves were expected to lower their gaze whenever their master looked at them. To make eye-to-eye contact was seen as a mark of insolence. I have been told by some of the older members of our African American fellowship that this same attitude existed in the South long after the abolition of slavery. The Jim Crow laws were meant to humiliate African Americans. Slavery *is* humiliation, so if Jesus was to be the *doulos* he would have to willingly experience the depths of humiliation.

Second, Paul sings that *Jesus became obedient.* This was radical obedience because it was "unto death." Perhaps it goes without saying, but obedience, willing or otherwise, was a fundamental expectation of the slave owner and a grim reality to the slave. There was no such thing as choice, no option to say "no" to any command, no matter how difficult or degrading. Slaves who were disobedient could expect to be punished severely, flogged, beaten and starved. Frederick Douglass explains that disobedient slaves were sent to "slave breakers." He himself was handed over to a cruel man named Edward Covey who, after months of abuse, succeeded in "breaking" Douglas's, who describes the aftermath: "The cheerful spark that lingered about my eye died; the dark night of slavery closed in upon me; and behold a man transformed into a brute!"

No one had to break Jesus. He came into the world a broken man, having let go of all his expectations, all the authority he might have wielded as the One who was equal with God. Yet he experienced all the cruelty, the humiliation and the beatings any slave in any age might have expected. The writer of Hebrews tells us that Jesus spoke upon coming into the world, "I have come to do Your will, O God" (Hebrews 10:7).

The hymn Paul sings to the Philippians contains only one dark verse (6-8) and one luminous chorus (9-11). The verse comes to a close with the darkest of all images—the cross. Crucifixion, says the Roman historian Tacitus, was seen as a slave's death. On the cross the full expression of his obedience and humility is made heartbreakingly visible.

This was their first song. It is a song about a man who dies like a slave. It is a song that is meant to be sung by slaves, for slaves endure by means of a song.

11

Slaves Who
Waited for the Way

Those slaves the master will find alert when he comes will be blessed.

LUKE 12:37

A GOOD SLAVE KNEW HOW TO WAIT. In the ancient world, as well as the world of the Americas, the picture of the solitary slave waiting noiselessly for the coming of the master is a familiar one. The Roman writer Seneca bemoans the state of the slave who must stand in one place all night. He could expect to be slapped if he even so much as coughed. Seneca writes, "All night long they must stand about, hungry and dumb." Likewise, Frederick Douglass tells a story of a young black girl who was given the responsibility of staying up all night with a sick infant. When she fell asleep, her mistress beat her to death.

The question remains open regarding just how many men and women were expectantly waiting for the Messiah when he finally arrived between 4 and 6 B.C. Even less settled is the question of what sort of Messiah they were waiting for.

In the Old Testament world, waiting was a unique expression of faith. Waiting for God to fulfill his promises, especially concerning the coming of the Messiah, was an act of faith. In the opening chapters of the Gospels at least three people expressed their faith by waiting for God to fulfill the promises he had made in the Torah. They were waiting for a Fulfiller, not a destroyer; a Redeemer, not a slayer of enemies; for One who was a keeper of promises. These three were alert and expectant. And each one of them found their common identity in slavery.

Mary, the "Slave of the Master"

"Look, I am the slave of the Master," said Mary (Luke 1:38, author's translation).

There is so much that Mary does not know. "How will this be?" she whispers in troubled amazement to the luminous messenger. What is happening to me? Where is my life going to end up? What will Joseph think?

Of all that she does not know, one thing seems perfectly clear to her. This perspective will help her navigate the deep waters into which the small vessel of her life is about to go. It will be the source of her disturbingly clear obedience. She perfectly articulates this fundamental reality by her response to the angel's troubling news. She literally responds, "I am the slave of the Master." In her own words, this is who she understands herself to be. "Behold," she says in effect, "Look *at me*. This is who I am."

Over the centuries different translations have tried to soften the intensity of the radical commitment reflected in the language of this teenager. The word Luke uses is *doule*, simply the feminine form of *doulos* or "slave" (compare 1 Samuel 1:11). Most translations render it "servant," or others the even softer "handmaiden." But Mary is affirming that she sees herself as a slave in every sense of the word. She is surrendering all her rights, all her hopes and dreams, even and especially here her own body, absolutely to the One she acknowledges as her *Kyrios*, or Master.

"Behold, the slave of the *Master*," she whispers, out of breath. *Kyrios*, usually translated "Lord," is clearly a word that reflects divinity. The best example of this is found in the Septuagint, the ancient Greek translation of the Old Testament, which uses *Kyrios* to translate the Hebrew personal name for God himself, a name that was so holy it was not even supposed to be spoken. Though the proper pronunciation has been lost, the closest rendering we have is "Yahweh." From this tradition many of our modern Old Testament translations still use the form "Lord" to express the connection to *Kyrios*.

But as we saw earlier, the word *Kyrios* has an older, original meaning—"owner." This nuance of the word is reflected in the translation "master," in the sense of someone who owns a slave. Having referred to herself in the same breath as a *doule*, it makes sense to translate *Kyrios* here as Master. Mary knows that she is owned by Another, and his ownership is absolute. Note well, Mary does not simply know that she is a slave; more importantly, she knows whose slave she is. Only this identity will give her the clarity and courage she will need to be the mother of Jesus.

Besides the extremity of their mutual suffering, African American slaves shared something else with those who identify themselves as slaves in the Gospels—singing. Frederick Douglass once noted that white slavers pointed to the singing of the slaves as evidence that their suffering was not that bad. Douglass countered, "We sang the most because we suffered the most."

Though my experience of suffering is nothing by comparison, in thirty years of singing and writing songs I have also found this to be true. Sorrow brushes up against the strings of the soul and brings songs that come no other way. Paul Laurence Dunbar was the son of slaves and the first African America poet to gain national acclaim. In one of his best-loved poems, "Sympathy," he states:

> I know why the caged bird sings, ah me,
> When his wing is bruised and his bosom sore,
> When he beats the bars and would be free;
> It is not a carol of joy or glee,
> But a prayer that he sends from his heart's deep core.

I find it deeply moving that Mary's first reply to the news of Gabriel is the typical response of a slave. She sings.

> And Mary said:
> My soul proclaims the greatness of the Lord,
> and my spirit has rejoiced in God my Savior,
> because He has looked with favor on the humble condition
>   of His slave.
> Surely, from now on all generations will call me blessed,
> because the Mighty One has done great things for me,
> and holy is His name.
> His mercy is from generation to generation on those who
>   fear Him.
> He has done a mighty deed with His arm;
> He has scattered the proud because of the thoughts
>   of their hearts;
> He has toppled the mighty from their thrones
> and exalted the lowly.
> He has satisfied the hungry with good things
> and sent the rich away empty.
> He has helped His servant Israel, mindful of His mercy,

just as He spoke to our ancestors,

to Abraham and his descendants forever. (Luke 1:46-55)

She sings about the humility of her slavery (v. 48), and she sings about the slavery of her people (v. 54). After all, it is an engrained part of her identity, derived from the identity of her people, who were slaves in Egypt.

I wonder, had she only known more, if she would have added a verse about her future Son who would define forever what it meant to live the life of a slave and find there the path to true freedom.

Her song has come to be known as the Magnificat. It is a song of praise, a song of worship, for Mary is celebrating the "worth" of God, of her Master. And only a slave who has renounced ownership of her body can truly worship (Romans 12:1). But there is between the lines a poignancy that is reminiscent of the Negro spirituals. They were also songs about bearing the burden of waiting, about the fact that waiting for deliverance can also be an act of faith.

Mary is a slave to an impossible demand, for the virgin to bear a Son. The call of God is always impossible. To impotent Abram and sterile Sarai he says, "Make a son." To the young virgin who sees herself simply as a slave kneeling at the feet of an angel he says, "You will have a Son." To become obedient to his call always means becoming a slave to the impossible. He asks us to do the impossible (like loving our enemies) knowing that the impossibility of the task will always drive us back to him, our Master, without whom even Jesus would say we can do nothing.

While I disagree with those who say Mary was perfect and somehow earned the privilege of bearing the Messiah, I affirm in the strongest terms that she was the perfect mother for Jesus.

Much of what made her perfect to be his mother was her self-understanding as a slave of the Master, a self-understanding she would imprint on her Son. Even more than her genetic contribution, perhaps his brown eyes or wavy hair, Mary contributed to the shape of his heart and life. Perhaps she even sang this song to him as a child, as she held him close, still trying to comprehend what it all meant. Who knows if, when he was washing the disciples' feet, he wasn't enacting something he had seen his mother do a thousand times.

SIMEON

Now, Master, You can dismiss Your slave in peace,
according to Your word. (Luke 2:29)

Simeon is a bridge between the worlds of the Old and New Testaments. In his world, having faith was expressed by waiting for God to act on his promises. In the New Testament world, with the coming of Jesus, faith would be expressed by following. Simeon faithfully waits in the old world, clinging to the particular promise God has made to him, that he would not die until he had seen the coming of the Messiah (Luke 2:26). Now, a very old man in a world where thirty was getting up there, he waits in the temple court, his hope still apparently strong. It may very well be the strongest part of him that's left.

When Simeon sees the infant Jesus he knows he is the one he's been waiting for. Taking the baby in his arms, like Mary before him, Simeon breaks into song. The Lord has kept the first part of his promise to Simeon; he has allowed him to see the Promised One. Now, Simeon sings, it is time to fulfill the second part of that promise and "let loose" his slave. That is, allow the elderly man to die.

So it is Simeon's death song, the Nunc Dimittis. But it is also a song of life and worship for all the people, embracing both Israel and the nations. It is an extremely short song, perhaps because that's all the breath Simeon has left.

He addresses his Master with the word *despota*, the word from which we get "despot" and "despotic." But none of these negative associations existed in the first century. The *despotes* was simply the possessor in distinction to the slave. Peter and Jude both refer to Jesus using the term (2 Peter 2:1; Jude 4). Some translations render it simply "Lord," others "Sovereign Lord." Like Mary's use of *kyrios* in connection to her self-designation as a slave, here *despota* should be translated to reflect the relationship between master and slave, between the owner and one who is willingly owned.

As an obedient servant, Simeon has one painful task left to do. He must share with Mary, his fellow servant, two words of promise. The first has to do with the nature of the ministry of her infant Son. He will cause the rising and falling of many in Israel and will be spoken against. It is the second word, however, which was undoubtedly the most painful to deliver to the young innocent girl: "A sword will pierce your own soul" (Luke 2:35).

Luke does not give us details of Mary's response to these troubling words about her son. He leaves us with the picture of Mary and Simeon standing there together, bonded together by a level of intimacy they both share as the slaves of the master, the old dying man and the young girl who has her whole life ahead of her. Between them Simeon holds Jesus, her infant baby, who will redeem the image of being a slave of God. He will redeem both of them standing there in the temple court, and will redeem the whole world, setting it free by become a slave himself.

JOHN THE BAPTIST

> Someone more powerful than I will come after me. I am not
> worthy to stoop down and untie the strap of His sandals.
> (Mark 1:7)

If Simeon stands on one side of the bridge between the Testaments, John the Baptist stands defiantly on the other. Simeon expressed his faith through waiting; John showed his faith by telling his own followers to follow Jesus instead.

It is difficult for us to realize just how famous the ministry of John was. Initially, it was far more successful than that of Jesus. In John 4:1 we read a hint of the pressure that was being applied to both of them from the Pharisees in terms of who was more popular. Jesus responds characteristically by leaving the area, apparently avoiding the custom of baptizing his disciples, as John had done. Likewise in the book of Acts we meet followers of John who still only know John's baptism (18:25). To this day, I am told, there is a sect that still worships John the Baptist as the Messiah.

An overview of the opening of the Gospel of John (written by another disciple of Jesus with the same name), reveals a virtual campaign to disconnect John the Baptist from any messianic pretensions his followers might still harbor. In chapter one, we hear John himself insisting three or more times that he is *not* the Messiah, nor is he connected with anyone associated with him, not with Elijah, nor Moses (the "prophet"). When the crowd insists on some kind of answer, John responds by quoting the prophet Isaiah 40:3. Given the context of the situation, of John's adamant refusal of any notoriety whatsoever, for the sake of tone I imagine him responding, "I am *only* a voice."

Before John reluctantly baptizes Jesus, for he acknowledges he is not worthy even to do that, he makes a final statement about himself that, though it does not contain the word *slave,* places John firmly in the waiting ranks of Mary and Simeon.

In Mark's Gospel, John says, "I am not worthy to loosen His sandal." (Matthew says even more humiliatingly, "I am not worthy to carry His sandal.") The detail of the loosing of the sandal naturally brings to mind the image of the slave, loosing the master's sandals at the end of the day. In the ancient world some Roman slaves' sole duty was dressing and undressing their masters. But John, speaking to a Jewish audience and more specifically to a pharisaic element within the group, has in mind a pronouncement of the rabbis: "All services which a slave does for his master a pupil should do for his teacher, with the exception of undoing his shoes."

In their zeal to serve their teacher-rabbis, rabbinic students were encouraged to do anything a slave would for his owner, except one thing that was seen as too humiliating—they could not loosen the sandal thong. When John the Baptist, amidst the adulation he receives as the first true prophet in Israel in four hundred years, makes this reference to loosening the sandals of Jesus he is saying in effect, "I am not worthy to even be his slave." It is significant that, years later, when Paul was preaching in the synagogue in Pisidian Antioch, this is the only detail he remembers of John the Baptist (Acts 13:25). It also strikes me that John would have been tremendously gratified to be remembered simply as the one who was unworthy to untie Jesus' shoe. The first human voice to announce the true dignity of Jesus, the first one to confess him as the Lamb of God, was a man who defined himself in terms of slavery.

For the rest of his ministry, Jesus would encounter men and women who decidedly did not want to understand themselves

as slaves nor submit to the easy yoke Jesus offered them.
Zebedee's wife, the mother of James and John, clearly had in
mind a different future for her sons. After all, what is wrong
with a mother wanting the best for her sons? Jesus is to be
crowned king as soon as he arrives in Jerusalem. So why should
she not ask for a seat (perhaps a throne?) on either side of his
throne for her boys?

Jesus patiently responds to her, "You don't know what you're
asking" (Matthew 20:22). Though it is not clear to them at the moment, it will become painfully clear in just a few days that waiting
at Jesus' right and left hand in Jerusalem are not thrones but
crosses, not glorification but a slave's death.

The indignant ten, along with Zebedee's two sons, need to understand what would take them a lifetime to live out, that the path to
greatness comes only through slavery. The "way up" is down in
Jesus' kingdom. He will prove it excruciatingly on Golgotha. The
basin and the towel, the cup of cold water and the cross will become their marks of authority, their royal badges of true greatness. All his life Jesus would live it out in front of them.

From the very beginning of his ministry Jesus revealed himself
as the Man for others. He had come, not to be served, but to serve
and to offer his own life as the payment, as the ransom, to purchase innumerable slaves to join him in serving the world, in
washing feet with the water of his Word, in feeding them the Bread
of Life. His formula for greatness could not have been more profoundly disturbing or simple:

> Whoever wants to become great among you must be your
> servant [diakonos] and whoever would be first among you
> must be your slave [doulos]. (Matthew 20:26-27)

As we seek to reimagine all that the call of slavery to Christ means, I encourage you to imagine yourself crossing a bridge in the remaining chapters. Mary and Simeon stand on the waiting side, encouraging you to cross over. On the far side is the madman from the desert, John. He is waving you over excitedly to the other side, the following side. He is gaunt and smiling and on fire. "The way has been prepared," he shouts. "Come now, cross over and follow!"

12

Parables of Slavery

JESUS PEOPLES HIS PARABLES WITH SLAVES. He tells an amazing number of stories involving them. He seems preoccupied with them in his storytelling, perhaps because he so radically identifies with them. Scholars count between thirty-three and fifty-seven parables, depending on how a parable is defined. Of those almost half contain a slave or slave-type character. (See appendix D.)

Jesus' parables take a simple metaphor (e.g., being a disciple is *like* becoming a slave) and extend it into a short story by means of characters and action. The Greek word *parabole* literally means to "throw beside." Beside the simple metaphorical lesson, Jesus "throws down" a story to make the ideas more accessible, more convicting and often more scandalous.

Two key characteristics of Jesus' stories prove to be exceptionally powerful in the slave parables. The first is *identification*. Jesus told his parables in such a way that when the listeners heard the story, they would inevitably identify with one or more characters in the plot. The parables of Jesus demand that we interact at the level of the imagination by aligning ourselves with someone in the story. Perhaps you see yourself as the father who had been waiting for his wayward son to return. Or maybe you are the woman who had lost her most precious treasure and is looking everywhere to find it.

A parable found in Matthew 21:45 contains a striking example of the power of identification. We are told that the Pharisees realized that Jesus had told this parable against them. That is, Jesus told the story deliberately in such a way that they identified with one of the characters in the story and were scandalized by the power of the parable.

The second engaging feature of Jesus' parables is their *lack of closure*. This is not to say the stories do not come to an end. The coin is found. The boy returns home. But what is almost always lacking is any sort of summing up at the end. When Jesus finishes the story he deliberately neglects to give the moral or the lesson. This demands that we enter into the story and decide for ourselves. Lack of closure is the greatest strength of Jesus' parables as well as their greatest weakness. Many listeners are simply unwilling to engage the stories with their imaginations. But for those who do, the parables become transformational. In freedom the hearer is allowed the space to conclude for themselves what the story means.

In his open and imaginative stories, Jesus looks at slaves from every angle. He contrasts the relationships between faithful and unfaithful slaves, between slaves with good and abusive masters. He compares slaves with hired workers and concludes in almost every parable that the slaves were more faithful, that it is preferable to serve because of obedience to the Master than because one is being paid. He pictures free men who act like slaves, are threatened with being sold into slavery or who ask to be made into slaves.

When you stop and think about it, Jesus' use of the image of slavery in the parables makes a lot of sense. Slaves provided an everyday example to which he could point. They were everywhere. They represented a clearly understandable image.

Since by definition every slave had a master, a lord, an owner, they provided the perfect exemplars for stories designed to instill in Jesus' disciples a new understanding of what it would cost to acknowledge Jesus as Master, Lord and Owner. Since slaves were answerable to their lord, lived under his unquestionable authority, they were living parables of what it meant to submit to the lordship of Jesus. They possessed nothing. They had virtually no rights, no expectations, could make no demands. They provided the perfect paradigm for what a follower of Jesus might expect from a life lived out in acknowledgement of Christ as Lord and Master. If we seek to understand what Jesus would say about the better freedom of slavery, all we need to do is look at a few of the slave parables.

THE UNFORGIVING SLAVE

> For this reason, the kingdom of heaven can be compared to a king who wanted to settle accounts with his slaves. (Matthew 18:23)

Some of Jesus' most engaging parables are spoken in response to specific situations. Often someone in the crowd will ask a question, to which Jesus responds, not with the simple answer they wanted, but with a story, a story with which they must interact in order to receive the answer. In the prologue to the parable of the unforgiving slave we read that Jesus has been instructing his disciples on how to deal with a brother who sins against you (Matthew 18:15-20). It is not difficult to imagine Peter standing to the side, scratching his head, trying to cope with the impossible demand of his Master's message. Peter had been in business for himself and had no doubt been swindled a time or two. He asks how many times he is supposed to forgive his brother, volunteering what seems to him the generous option of seven times. In response Jesus tells a story of three men who were caught up in the same dilemma as Peter: How do you forgive someone who is unforgivable? This is the setting of the parable of the unforgiving slave.

The point of Jesus' response is not the math. The correct answer to how many times one must offer forgiveness is not 490! His response could be paraphrased, "Not just seven, but more times than you could possibly imagine" (see Genesis 4:24). Then comes the parable, the story that Jesus "throws down" in front of Peter to engage his imagination and invite him to understand forgiveness from a completely different point of view, from the viewpoint of a slave. If Peter will open his heart and mind to the story and engage with his imagination, his thinking on the subject of forgiveness will never be the same.

There were two slaves, Jesus says. One owed his master a million dollars, the other owed his fellow slave by comparison a much smaller sum. In order to pay off the enormous debt of the first, the king had made the calculated decision to sell the man's wife and children. This "indentured servitude" was how many people came into slavery in the ancient world.

When the first slave heard what was about to happen to his innocent family, he fell on his knees and asked the king for an extension, for more time to pay the debt. In an amazing demonstration of mercy, the king canceled the debt entirely. He went beyond the request for an extension; he magnanimously wiped the slate clean. This sort of over-the-top mercy is a frequent element in Jesus' parables. The father of the prodigal son doesn't just give the boy a second chance; he throws a magnificent feast. The Samaritan doesn't just stop and give the injured man a drink; he loads him on his own donkey, tends his wounds, pays the hotel bill and promises to come back to make sure everything is covered. Every time Jesus presents this kind of extravagant mercy he is painting a picture of his Father. In the Hebrew Bible *hesed* ("mercy" or "loving-kindness") is the defining characteristic of God.

Next comes the exchange between the two slaves. If we were fully engaged with our imaginations we might expect the slave who had his million-dollar debt canceled to also show mercy to his fellow slave. But Jesus' parables never give us what we expect. The one who had his million-dollar debt canceled finds his fellow slave and grabs him by the throat. After assaulting the poor man who owed him by comparison a far less sum, he throws him into prison, where he must stay until the debt is paid (v. 30).

When the king finds out (by means of the other slaves) about the unforgiving, unmerciful slave, he reverses his decision and orders him thrown into prison until his debt is paid, which we might well imagine would be the rest of his life.

"Shouldn't you have shown *mercy*?" the outraged king says to the wicked slave. (We can only assume that the king saw to it that the second slave was released from prison.) If mercy should be shown by anyone, says Jesus' story, it should be shown between people who know themselves to be slaves. Once you have received radical forgiveness, you are obliged to demonstrate it to others.

Jesus reshaped and retold his favorite stories. In Luke 7:41 a different version of this same parable appears. The setting is different; Jesus was attending a party in the home of a Pharisee named Simon. When a "sinful" woman came and washed his feet with her repentant tears, she became a living parable, an example of someone who had been forgiven the equivalent of a million-dollar debt of sin. Unlike the unforgiving slave in Jesus' parable, she responded differently to her Master's mercy. The love she lavishes on Jesus is accordingly extravagant and over the top. Both Simons, Peter and the Pharisee at the party, badly needed to learn this lesson about responding to the mercy of their Master by lavishing forgiveness on others. Peter would come to realize that he was obliged to offer forgiveness to the one who sinned against him an unimaginable number of times because his Master, Jesus, had canceled his million-dollar debt of sin. It is an understanding that only comes when one imagines oneself as the slave of an unimaginably merciful Master.

Dissimilar Masters at the Table

No one refers more to slaves than Luke, which should not surprise us since he was almost certainly once a slave himself. He has a slave name and a slave's profession. We know little about Luke's life as a slave. We know he was a doctor (Colossians 4:14), which virtually assures the fact that he was a slave, since the vast majority of physicians in the first century were slaves. We can tell from his writing that he had the compassion of a good doctor. He exhibits a wonderful sensitivity to the lives of slaves and outcasts in his Gospel.

Unlike the other Gospels, Luke almost always gives us the contexts of the parables, where Jesus was, what the complexion of the crowd was like. Luke is also unique in that he frequently shows us the parables actually working (7:16-21; 10:25). Of all the Gospel writers, Luke loves parables most, and he records more than thirty of them for us.

Having experienced at least one master in his previous life, perhaps more, it is interesting that only Luke includes in his Gospel the contrasting parables of two masters. One acts precisely as everyone would have expected a slave owner to act; the other is a master who acts in a way Luke's first hearers would have found almost unimaginable.

For effect, I would like to reverse the order of the parables and look at the second master first. Luke 17:7-10 provides a revealing glimpse into the world of first-century slavery. Jesus had been talking once more about the demands of forgiving a brother who sins against you. Sensing that they lack the faith to live up to such an impossible demand, the disciples ask Jesus to increase their faith (v. 5). In order to help them understand how to live forgivingly, Jesus tells yet another parable about a master and slave. In this story the master is acting exactly as we might expect a slave owner to act:

> Which one of you having a slave plowing or tending sheep, will say to him when he comes in from the field, "Come at once and sit down to eat"? Instead, will he not tell him, "Prepare something for me to eat, get ready, and serve me while I eat and drink; later you can eat and drink"? Does he thank that slave because he did what was commanded? In the same way, when you have done all that you were commanded, you should say, "We are good-for-nothing slaves; we've only done our duty." (Luke 17:7-10)

The point of the parable is, as slaves of Jesus we are to offer forgiveness in the same way the slave in the parable plowed or shepherded. We do not accrue extra points for doing what we are supposed to do. If seven times a day our brother sins against us, it is our duty, as slaves of Christ, to offer the same extravagant, over-the-top mercy that our Master first offered to us. Don't be offended by the term "good-for-nothing slaves." The fact is a slave's true worth is derived from his Master, from the One who owns us. At the end of the day, when our Master returns, we will have the privilege of further serving him. And that will be our reward. The disciples requested that Jesus "increase" their faith. The parable points to the truth that it is not more faith we need, but a deeper sense of identity with our Master, Jesus.

In the second parable, Jesus paints the picture of a master who does not behave at all like a typical *kyrios*. In fact he acts precisely the opposite of the master in the previous parable.

> Those slaves the master will find alert when he comes will be blessed. I assure you: He will get ready, have them recline at the table, then come and serve them. (Luke 12:37)

Luke loves to focus on the theme of radical reversal in the teaching and ministry of Jesus. It begins with the blessings and woes of chapter 6; the poor will possess a kingdom, the hungry will be satisfied and those who were weeping will laugh. All the while the well fed will hunger and those who were laughing will mourn. Everything will be turned upside down by the coming of Jesus. And Luke the slave is delighted by the prospect.

In chapter 12, almost hidden away in a veiled discussion about his second coming, Jesus tells a short story about a remarkable moment of radical reversal between a master and his slaves. If you aren't reading closely, you'll pass right over verse 37 and miss this extraordinary image.

"Be dressed, ready for service," Jesus tells his disciples in 12:35-36, "like those who are waiting for their *Kyrios*." When the Master returns from the wedding banquet, Jesus tells them, he is going to knock on the door. If you are ready to serve him at this moment something unheard of is going to happen to you. Even as he encouraged you to be dressed for service, so Jesus says in verse 37, the Master will dress himself to serve. He will invite his ready slaves to recline at the table and wait on them. This *Kyrios* is acting in an unheard of way, or is he? Is there not something in this story that sounds familiar?

In John 13:4-5, Jesus did exactly what the master in the parable in Luke did; he took off his outer cloak, wrapped a towel around himself (i.e., "dresses himself to serve") and moved around the table, washing the feet of the Twelve. Clearly, the image in the parable of the Serving Master in Luke was lived out by Jesus in the footwashing of John chapter 13. The story in Luke prophetically refers to what John in Revelation calls the "wedding supper of the Lamb" (19:7). It hints at a remarkable fact: that at the wedding supper of the Lamb, Jesus will do what he did in John 13. *He will amaze his servants by waiting on those slaves who were ready to wait on him.*

Two completely different masters—one who reminds us it is simply our duty to serve and forgive, another who compassionately serves us a meal to celebrate our obedience and expectation of his return.

THE WISE AND WICKED SLAVE

Who then is a faithful and sensible slave, whom his master has put in charge of his household, to give them food at the proper time? That slave whose master finds him working when he comes will be rewarded. I assure you: He will put him in charge of all his possessions. But if that wicked slave says in his heart, "My master is delayed," and starts to beat his fellow slaves, and eats and drinks with drunkards, that slave's master will come on a day he does not expect and at an hour he does not know. (Matthew 24:45-50)

Matthew 24 and 25 contain the longest continuous teaching by Jesus on the end times. The lengthy lesson comes in response to a two-part question from the disciples. First they ask, "When will these things happen?" and then "What is the sign of Your coming and of the end of the age?" (24:3). Earlier, in chapter 23, just three days before the crucifixion, Jesus had exploded for the second time in the temple area (see John 2:13-22). What began as a slow simmer (Matthew 23:2-12) boiled over into the "woes" directed at the Pharisees and teachers of the law. Jesus' language explodes in verses 32-36; it is the language of rage. But in 37-39, his heart breaks into a lament over Jerusalem.

His disciples had never seen him so unhinged. They are shaken by the sight. On the way out of the temple area, they try to make small talk, diverting Jesus' attention to the large foundation stones he has seen a thousand times. But Jesus will have nothing to do with small talk. "It is all going to be pulled down; not one stone will be left on top of another," he tells them, regaining his composure. That sobering statement marks the end of Jesus' public teaching ministry. From now on he will only speak to the disciples in private conversations. Clearly this last statement frightens and confuses them.

In response to their two-part question, Jesus speaks of the coming destruction of A.D. 70, when Titus and his Roman legions will literally not leave one stone of the temple left on another. Jesus describes an historical event, something that someone can run away from. This is the answer to their first question (Matthew 24:4-28). Then comes a lengthy, apocalyptic answer to the second part of their question about the end of the age. Jesus tells them this is something from which they cannot run. It is the end of the world (vv. 29-41).

After the day they've had, after the horrific news they've just heard, Jesus senses it is time for a story. Having heard the unimaginable images of the coming of the end of the world, the disciples need to hear about some images they can imagine. So Jesus tells them about a simple slave.

He has two choices, this slave. He can be faithful and wise, and care for his Master's household while he is away, or he can forget about his Master. It will be good for him if he is found serving when the Master returns. If the disciples of Jesus were wondering what in the world they could possibly do to prepare for fulfillment of his devastating prophecies, the answer of the parable is to be found serving when he returns. The only way to be ready is to be a faithfully serving slave.

For the servant in the story who forgets the Master, Jesus paints an image as unimaginable as his earlier apocalyptic images. The servant who acts as if he were a master, who beats his fellow slaves, eating and drinking instead of serving them as he was tasked to do, will be cut in two and sent to hell.

Contrast the outcomes of the two slaves. For the first, Jesus simply says, "It will be good." It is an echo perhaps of "Well done." But for the second, whose master returns when the disobedient slave does not expect, the image is of the same kind of unspeakable devastation Jesus prophesied for Jerusalem.

Jesus began the parable by saying that the Son of Man would return "at an hour when you do not expect Him" (v. 44). The unexpectedness of his return, therefore, is a given. In verse 36 Jesus mysteriously says that even he does not know the hour. So what are the disciples to do? What are we to do? In the face of the unimaginable, apocalyptic images, in light of the fact that it is going to happen when we least expect it, Jesus gives us the simplest of images and clear, uncomplicated instructions. Serve as only a faithful slave would. Don't wait and watch the sky—wash feet. Don't get caught up in calculations of when the "end time" is coming—offer the cup of cold water. Like the slave in Jesus' parable, the choice is ours.

THE SUFFERING SLAVES

Listen to another parable: There was a man, a landowner, who planted a vineyard, put a fence around it, dug a winepress in it, and built a watchtower. He leased it to tenant farmers and went away. When the grape harvest drew near, he sent his slaves to the farmers to collect his fruit. But the farmers took his slaves, beat one, killed another, and stoned a third. Again, he sent other slaves, more than the first group, and they did the same to them. Finally, he sent his son to them. "They will respect my son," he said.

But when the tenant farmers saw the son, they said among themselves, "This is the heir. Come, let's kill him and take his inheritance!" So they seized him and threw him out of the vineyard, and killed him. Therefore, when the owner of the vineyard comes, what will he do to those farmers?

"He will completely destroy those terrible men," they told Him, "and lease his vineyard to other farmers who will give him his produce at the harvest."

Jesus said to them, "Have you never read in
    the Scriptures:

The stone that the builders rejected
has become the cornerstone.
This came from the Lord
and is wonderful in our eyes?

Therefore I tell you, the kingdom of God will be taken away from you and given to a nation producing its fruit. Whoever falls on this stone will be broken to pieces; but on whomever it falls, it will grind him to powder!

When the chief priests and the Pharisees heard His parables, they knew He was speaking about them. Although they were looking for a way to arrest Him, they feared the crowds, because they regarded Him as a prophet. (Matthew 21:33-46)

This parable occurs shortly after Jesus disrupted the marketplace in the temple for the second and final time. Understandably, after that event Jewish leaders questioned his authority to have done something so disruptive. It is interesting that no one questioned whether what Jesus did was right or not. They all understood that it needed to be done. The only real question was one of authority.

But their question of authority was a trick and a trap. They did not really want an answer but incriminating evidence. If Jesus answered that his authority came from God he would be charged with blasphemy. If he said it had come from men, they would have accused him of fomenting revolution against Rome. Jesus responded to their loaded question, as he always did, with another, harder question. For the moment, they are silenced and so Jesus tells two parables, the second concerning faithful slaves.

In verse 33, Jesus begins the story of a vine grower who created an entire winemaking facility (compare John 15 and Isaiah 5). Not only did he plant the vineyard, he walled it in, built a protective watchtower and constructed a winepress. The whole operation was ready; now it only required capable workers. It is significant that Jesus introduces hired workers at this point in the story. These are not his slaves; they are wage earners, who will profit from the produce of the wine factory and pay rent to the owner.

When the harvest came, the owner sent some of his slaves to collect what was due him. One of the slaves was severely beaten, one killed, another stoned. Next the owner sent a larger force of slaves, but the same thing happened to them. Finally the owner, perhaps naively but not unreasonably sent his own son, hoping the tenants would respect his authority. But the son they also killed. The story is a wonderfully constructed trap, and now Jesus invites the very ones who had tried to ensnare him earlier to step inside.

"When the owner of the vineyard returns, what do you think he will do to the tenants?"

Taking the bait hook, line and sinker, the religious leaders erupt in outrage. The owner will "bring those wretches to a wretched end!" they shout. When Luke tells the same story he adds that they shouted, "May this never happen!" (20:16).

Jesus springs the trap with the rabbinic phrase, "Have you never read?" You can almost see the color draining from their faces as he quotes Psalm 118:22. It refers to an incident that occurred when the temple was first constructed. A stone that had been rejected during the building of the foundations was later used as one of the keystones for the porch, the most visible part of the temple.

The parable's power of identification ensnares the Pharisees. Matthew tells us, "They knew Jesus was talking about them" (v.

45). They were the distant disobedient wage earners who were intent on killing the son in the parable. As a result they began to look for a way to arrest him, simply because Jesus had told them a story about an "owner" (*kyrios*) whose obedient slaves and innocent son were murdered by some ungrateful hirelings. In a similar story Jesus speaks of hired shepherds who do not take care of the flock (John 10:12).

In this tale, the slaves are in league with the son. They are one. They suffer for and with him. Some of them even die for him. They had no expectations. They knew that none of the profit of the harvest belonged to them. They simply obeyed the command of the master, even when it meant they would fight what seemed a losing battle.

In the prologue to the story Jesus makes it clear that the principal character in the story is not as helpless as he might seem. Though rejected, he is nonetheless the chosen Stone. He will someday come crashing down on those who threaten his servants.

Who Is the Real Slave?

Now his older son was in the field; as he came near the house, he heard music and dancing. So he summoned one of the servants and asked what these things meant. "Your brother is here," he told him, "and your father has slaughtered the fattened calf because he has him back safe and sound."

Then he became angry and didn't want to go in. So his father came out and pleaded with him. But he replied to his father, "Look, I have been slaving many years for you, and I have never disobeyed your orders, yet you never gave me a young goat so I could celebrate with my friends." (Luke 15:25-29)

We don't often think of it as a slave parable, but slavery is hidden in the heart of the story of the prodigal son. Luke makes a point to tell us that Jesus was speaking to a mixed crowd (15:1-2). There were the "sinners" and there were the so-called saints (i.e., the Pharisees). To this divided group Jesus tells three parables about "lost-ness." In actuality the first two stories, of the lost sheep and coin, are really only preludes to the main story of the lost son. Some people call this the greatest of Jesus' parables for its perfect depiction of the *hesed* of the Father. It is a story he specifically crafted for the mixed crowd. Though you might think it is a simple matter to see which of the two sons was lost, it might not be as simple as you think. Jesus' stories never are.

If you read the parables of Jesus long enough you will come to expect the fact that nothing is as it seems. The world of his listeners is always about to be turned upside down. If you listen with your imagination fully engaged, your world just might be turned upside down as well.

The case of the younger brother is a relatively simple one. He has blown it all, forfeited everything and upon realizing it has returned home to ask for forgiveness. He rehearses a lame little speech along the way. Realizing that he is no longer worthy to be called a son, he is willing to become a hired hand (*misthios*). That is his plea, only he never gets the chance to finish his little speech because his father envelopes the prodigal with hugs, kisses and gifts, breathlessly dragging him off to an extravagant party given in his honor.

The case of the older brother is much more complex, much more interesting and just maybe more to the point. It is too bad we so rarely take a look at him. He is standing in the shadows for most of the story. He is bitter, envious and angry. He hates his brother's sin but he also hates his father's loving forgiveness. Keeping in mind the confession of his broken brother, listen to his bitter words in verse 29. Literally he says, "I have been *slaving* for you" *(douleuo)*.

Do you see the irony Jesus intended the mixed crowd to perceive? The prodigal (the "sinner") returns in repentance and says, "I will be your hireling." The older son (the Pharisee) retorts in bitterness, "I have been a slave all along!"

In the first two of the three parallel "lost parables" the person found a lost but valuable possession, a lost sheep and lost coin. The first two stories conclude, "There is more joy . . . over one sinner who repents." The final story, of the two sons, lacks this verbal conclusion; it shows us the party. In the third parable it is left to us to decide which of the sons was really lost or found. Clearly there was a party for the first one. Jesus leaves it open as to whether there will ever be a second party, whether the son who was slaving will ever realize that he is truly a son. Lack of closure invites us to interact with our imaginations to see if we can possibly imagine a God who is Father enough to celebrate the return of the second son.

WELL DONE

For it is just like a man going on a journey. He called his own slaves and turned over his possessions to them. To one he gave five talents; to another, two; and to another, one—to each according to his own ability. Then he went on a journey. Immediately the man who had received five talents went, put them to work, and earned five more. In the same way the man with two earned two more. But the man who had received one talent went off, dug a hole in the ground, and hid his master's money.

After a long time the master of those slaves came and settled accounts with them. The man who had received five talents approached, presented five more talents, and said, "Master, you gave me five talents. Look, I've earned five more talents."

His master said to him, "Well done, good and faithful slave! You were faithful over a few things; I will put you in charge of many things. Share your master's joy!"

Then the man with two talents also approached. He said, "Master, you gave me two talents. Look, I've earned two more talents."

His master said to him, "Well done, good and faithful slave! You were faithful over a few things; I will put you in charge of many things. Share your master's joy!"

Then the man who had received one talent also approached and said, "Master, I know you. You're a difficult man, reaping where you haven't sown and gathering where you haven't scattered seed. So I was afraid and went off and hid your talent in the ground. Look, you have what is yours."

But his master replied to him, "You evil, lazy slave! If you knew that I reap where I haven't sown and gather where I haven't scattered, then you should have deposited my money with the bankers. And when I returned I would have received my money back with interest.

"So take the talent from him and give it to the one who has 10 talents. For to everyone who has, more will be given, and he will have more than enough. But from the one who does not have, even what he has will be taken away from him. And throw this good-for-nothing slave into the outer darkness. In that place there will be weeping and gnashing of teeth." (Matthew 25:14-30)

Of all the horrific and heartbreaking stories of African American slavery, one of the most pathetic is Frederick Douglass's remembrance of the first time a white person ever smiled at him. It occurred when he first arrived in Baltimore and involved his new master's wife, Sophie Auld. Though her disposition would soon revert to the cruelty that was customary, the moment was luminous for Douglass. I suppose it surprised him because he never imagined it was possible to receive any encouragement from a white person, much less a simple smile or an encouraging, "Well done."

In one of his final parables in Matthew's Gospel, Jesus, sitting on the Mount of Olives, tells his disciples a story about three slaves who were entrusted with an enormous treasure. The first was given five thousand dollars, the second more than two thousand and the third over a thousand. Jesus is careful to note that each slave was given the money according to his ability. The master knew what to expect from each one, so the most talented was entrusted with the largest sum of money and so on. In the parable the master departs, as Jesus will also shortly do.

We are given not a single detail of how the first two slaves generated their profits. Apparently, Jesus did not think the flow of the story needed the extra detail. What is significant is that each slave performed precisely according to the master's expectations. The one who had been given five generated five more, while the one with two earned two more. The third slave simply buried the money in the ground where no one would steal it. Though the master expected the least from the third slave, he is still disappointed.

Upon his return the slaves are called in to settle their accounts. Notice that the size of their accomplishments does not affect the amount of praise they receive. Though one generated more than twice the profit of the other, they both hear the same "Well done."

Not so with the third slave. He has no profit to bring. "Here is what belongs to you," he tells his master as he hands back the single talent. For him it was not a simple matter of obedience or disobedience, as it was for the other two. It was a matter of fear. "I was afraid," he says, "for you are a hard man." Fear is the opposite of faith. The slave's fear is rooted in the fact that he did not really know the character of his master.

The first two slaves acted without question, since a slave does not have the choice. "Here is the gift, now serve according to your ability." The command of the Lord is just that simple. The master never asked the slaves, "Do you feel like doing this?" Imagine the disturbing clarity that would fall on the church if the question "Do I like it?" or "Do I feel like doing it?" simply disappeared. What would the church look like if we returned to the "lowliness of mind" of the slave? Not what does the world desire or need, not what would attract the most people, but only, "What does the Master command?"

The slave parables of Jesus teach us that, beyond all doubt, the Master is not a "hard man," but rather one of immeasurable mercy, someone who cancels million-dollar debts with the wave of his hand. He is the Master who dresses himself to serve and wash the feet of his slaves. He is the One who is willing to suffer and die with and for his servants. But finally, and it must be said, he is a Lord who expects simple, trusting obedience, not based on wage or reward but simply on the knowledge of who our Master is. Who does not long to be in the service of such a Lord?

A LESSON ON A LAWN MOWER

I spent a couple of hours this morning with one of my best friends,

Denny. He died three months ago. I called his wife, Lelia, the night before to see how she was holding up. At the end of a long conversation (during which she uttered not a word of complaint) she mentioned that the lawn was beginning to get a bit out of hand. I had nothing to do that morning and had just bought a shiny new "zero turn" mower, so I promised to take care of it for her.

As I unloaded the machine I recalled the times I'd spent in that yard with Denny. The first occasion was helping him spread a truckload of topsoil. I drove the tractor into town, and under his watchful eye I did my best to spread the soil evenly. We hadn't been friends long. As he stood, leaning on a shovel, I tried to make a joke, something like, "Isn't it always the same, the white man driving the machinery and the black man left with the shovel."

Denny's steely glance back told me that we hadn't been friends long enough for such jokes. Maybe we would never be friends that long.

I remembered years later nervously watching him deep-fry a mountain of pork chops for his grandsons, an enormous vat of grease over an open flame. When I tried to warn Denny of the possible danger he retorted, "I'm too old a cat to be scratched by a kitten like you."

As I began to make circles around the yard, I met memories at each go around. I could hear his voice, *Is that how your Daddy taught you to mow a lawn?*

There is no greater affirmation junkie than me. I hunger and feed on and soak up every crumb of compliment that comes my way. But I must confess that I never needed nor wanted a thank you from Denny. He never seemed to expect one from me.

"Don't break your arm patting yourself on the back," my mother used to say to me whenever I fished for affirmation. Occasionally, as I circle the yard I meet her too. She died the same day Denny died.

It's a good thing that it takes two hands to steer my new "zero turn" or else I just might throw out my bad shoulder trying to pat myself on the back this morning. I am quoting verses to myself about caring for widows and orphans, pondering just how lucky Jesus is that I'm on his team.

A little more than a week before he died, I was stranded at an auto repair shop and needed a ride home. After calling everyone else, I tried Denny's cell. "Pastor Denson," his usual answer, though his voice was definitely fading. He was shopping a couple of miles down the road.

"When you're finished, could you swing by and—"

"I'll drop what I'm doing and come now," he interrupted.

In two minutes he was there, looking wan and tired. I launched into an apologetic list only to hear him say, "You don't need to thank me. This is what brothers do, right?"

And he was right. This is what brothers, sisters, servants do.

I can't remember anyone ever saying thank you to Jesus, except the one Samaritan leper (Luke 17:15). From the five thousand, the four thousand and the disciples he fed and cared for, not a word. Jesus did not wait for them to thank him after he washed their feet. Nor does he seem especially disappointed when they do not. And it's a good thing too.

Servants don't stand around and wait for thanks or affirmation when they do their duty. Everything they do is a privilege when it is done for their Master.

13

The Servant Savior

IT IS NOT DIFFICULT TO IMAGINE those other major images of Jesus, the ones we often hear preached about and sung. It is easy, even comforting to enter into them at the level of the imagination—the baby in the cattle trough, the peripatetic teacher on the road to Jerusalem, the firebrand overturning the tables in the temple court. Even the unimaginable image of the crucifixion seems readily available to our mind's eye. But the image of the Servant Savior is different, and more difficult.

When we seek to imagine Jesus' role as a slave, the immediate passage that comes to mind is the washing of the disciples' feet in John 13. Most often we focus on the moment when Jesus dresses himself to serve and slowly, wordlessly, makes his way around the three-sided table (triclinium) washing the dumbfounded disciples' feet just as the "sinful" woman had earlier washed his feet with her tears when Jesus reclined at the table with Simon the Pharisee (Luke 7), or Mary had anointed him a few days earlier (John 12).

Or we narrow the focus to Jesus and Peter alone, the central characters of the scene. We are attracted by the energy field that surrounds both of them as it arcs back and forth between Peter's clueless refusals and Jesus' relentless obedience to his calling of taking the very nature of a slave (Philippians 2:6-11). He knows it is the only cure for their stubborn refusal to become his disciples in the truest sense of the word, to follow in his footsteps wherever they might lead.

For us, now is the time to reimagine the scene from a wider perspective. We must include Jesus' words immediately preceding the disturbing event, as John remembers them for us in his aged imagination. In addition, perhaps more importantly, we need to look at the context provided by the lengthy passage recorded only by Luke immediately after the footwashing.

For reasons we will never be able to determine, Luke the former slave cannot bring himself to tell the humiliating story of the washing of the disciples' feet. Or perhaps he could not find an eyewitness who was willing to tell the story. Luke 22 provides the vital context for the John 13 story—there had been an argument.

Luke tells us in his great central section called the travel narrative (because it tells the story of the final journey to Jerusalem and the cross) that along the way on more than one occasion the disciples had argued about which one of them was the greatest. It was an argument that began back in Capernaum (Mark 9:33-37), when Jesus used a little child, perhaps even the daughter of Peter, as an example for the bickering disciples. Luke tells us the disciples were arguing among themselves about who was the greatest. And this was not the first time such an argument had broken out among the disciples (Luke 9:46; compare Matthew 18:1; 23:11; Mark 9:34). It is not hard to imagine Peter and the others occasionally putting in their oar, reminding Jesus of who loves him most or who left behind the most or maybe even who had been following the longest.

Later on the road to Jerusalem, James and John, apparently with the encouragement of their mother, fed the fire and asked for places at Jesus' right and left hand. They did not understand that they were asking for crosses, so Jesus refuses them for the moment. Ironically it seems to me, the two brothers would be the first and the last of the disciples to die for him.

At last, they reach the goal of their long and emotional journey—Jerusalem. After a week of conflict they come to the final meal, the meal that begins with Jesus' passionate confession, "I have fervently desired to eat this Passover with you" (Luke 22:15). Meanwhile, the disciples are bickering like spoiled schoolboys. Jesus is calling them to a level of maturity and intimacy with him they could hardly imagine. We might be tempted to wonder what maturing effect spending three years with Jesus had on the disciples. Just how much impact did Jesus' powerful personality and personal example have on them anyway?

It is a pivotal moment in the ministry. There is precious little time left. In a matter of hours Jesus will be arrested, bound and dragged away from them. It is difficult to determine just what they have absorbed and what remains left to sink into their stubborn hearts. Undeniably the lesson of obedience to the call of slavery has not entered into either their hearts or their imaginations.

It is a pivotal moment in another sense as well, in that Jesus finally gives up on words. He has told them numerous parables about slaves, now he will portray the most humiliating of slave roles, the washing of feet. Even after three long years of his often bizarre and indescribable behavior, the disciples are befuddled by the inappropriate behavior that leaves them speechless.

After the washing of their feet and the emotional exchange with Peter, Jesus dresses himself and resumes his place at the end of the three-sided table. By now Judas has disappeared on his dark errand.

"Do you have any idea what I have just done for you? Can you imagine?" he asks the stunned disciples. "I am your teacher. What's more, I am your Master *[kyrios]*." The words of Jesus that follow are held by some denominations to have a sacramental character, resulting in the belief that footwashing should be regarded as a sacrament of the church. "Since I your Lord and Master have washed your feet, you should wash each other's feet. I have given you an example. Do as I have done, since a slave is not greater than his master nor is the one who is sent *[apostolos]* greater than the one who sends him" (John 13:14-16, author's translation).

The slave as the "sent one" or apostle has frequent parallels in the New Testament (Matthew 8:9; Mark 12:2; Luke 2:29; Acts 3:26). This connection is further strengthened in light of the frequent parallelism that exists between the words for slave and apostle (Romans 1:1; Titus 1:1; 2 Peter 1:1). To be a slave frequently means to be sent out on an errand or mission, to be the apostle.

John 13 tells the story of Jesus washing the disciples' feet, but only Luke tells us what caused it. The historian Josephus said that a free person acting as a slave was shameful. Only John, all those years later, had the courage to finally paint the pitiful picture of the glorious Messiah on his knees washing the dirty feet of his status-seeking disciples.

Jesus knows the time is short and this, of all the lessons he has tried to impart to them, is the most important. Jesus appeals to their identity as Jewish men, saying, "Don't be like the Gentiles," who simply use good works to gain the social position of "benefactor." In the Roman world men would climb the political/ social ladder (the *cursus honorum*) by acts of public generosity, through donations to temples or public works projects. When you tour ancient ruins from the Roman period, every fountain, every gate, even every lavatory bears an inscription of the benefactor who donated the money for the project. Julius Caesar began his climb to power through such acts of "charity" to the point of virtual bankruptcy.

Jesus' command calls for the opposite mindset. His slaves would not serve in order to be "seen of men" (see chapter 6 on "eye-slavery"). "But not so with you," Jesus says. I imagine him pouring water into the basin, moving toward the bewildered disciples with a towel draped over his arm. This is the new definition of greatness. Jesus says, "I am among you as one who *serves*," and here Luke uses the word from which we get our word *deacon*. Jesus' wordless answer to the argument about who is the greatest is to assume the posture of a slave. Is it the one who reclines at the table or the one who serves? Kneeling played no role in either Greek or Roman religious practices. It was seen as "slavish behavior." Yet as he kneels before them one at a time, slowly making his way around the table toward stubborn Peter, the answer is unavoidable. And as far as we know, the disciples never argued about who was the greatest ever again.

John opens the account of the footwashing by telling us that this was how Jesus showed "the full extent of his love" (John 13:1 NIV). Love and humiliation. The two go hand in hand. Sometimes this combination is all that can keep us going, whether in a friendship, a marriage or in the life of the church. "The best way to learn humility," said Mother Teresa, "is to be humiliated."

HUMILITY INCARNATE: A TRIBUTE

When I imagine the words *humility* or *humiliation* and how love can be expressed through them, my mind always travels back to one person. Her name was Mary Lizzy Eddings, and she was the first woman I ever loved. She came to work in our house the week before I was born and remained a part of our family for over thirty years until she died. She was large, black and indomitable, loving in her own concentrated way long before anyone was talking about "tough love." I don't think Mary could have imagined any other kind of love.

Her grandfather was a slave, and she could remember picking cotton in Georgia as a very young girl alongside men and women who had been slaves. She would smile and tell how occasionally she would put a rock in the sack that was slung around her neck so that the bag would come up to the required weight sooner. She remembered being so hungry that she once ate a shoebox of red Georgia clay just to have something in her stomach. She never learned to drive, since the first time she tried she drove her boy-friend's Model T into a pond. Her mind was shut on the subject, so she never drove.

From the time I was a newborn, she was a powerful, steady presence in my life. As I began to sit up and eat in a high chair she prided herself on being the only person who could make me eat anything. "Boy, you'd better open up that mouth," she would say sternly but not threateningly. She had authority, I knew she had authority, she knew that I knew and that was that. She told me later, "Then you'd smile and open your mouth just like a little bird." Deep sonorous laughter followed, and in later years a tear or two. When I was six or seven she accidentally came into by bedroom with an armload of clean clothes. When I screamed with the newfound modesty of a seven-year-old she quipped, "Boy, I saw you before you saw yourself."

When I was old enough, she would always have me walk her to the door, like a date. I actually proposed to her when I was five. It all made perfect sense to me. She could live with us and take care of me. More deep laughter and tears and knee slapping.

I grew up following Mary like a puppy throughout the house as she worked away at the endless, thankless routines of housework. The only time she would stay in one place for very long was when she ironed. Then I would sit beside her on the countertop and ask for stories, my favorites, which I could ask for by name. "Tell the one about the pond and the Model T," I'd say. Sometimes she would tell stories I hadn't asked for, heartbreaking stories of the discrimination and prejudice she experienced in the 1960s and '70s in the racially charged city of Nashville.

She told one story in particular over and over again. It had no impact on my mind then, but I nevertheless listened politely, since I simply loved hearing the sound of her voice. When she first moved to Nashville she had worked in the home of a white woman whose name I remember but will not record. One day the woman asked Mary to wash the windows, a chore she was happy to do. After she finished, she asked Mary to go back in the yard, break some twigs off a large bush, chew up the ends of the twigs and use them to clean the corners of the windowpanes.

Of all her humiliating experiences, this was the story Mary repeated most often. I wonder if it was an experience that made her feel the humiliation of a slave. She refused to chew the branches to clean the glass and was summarily fired. "She can clean her own windows," she said. Then more laughter, perhaps victorious laughter, but not a drop of guile.

I am about to say something I hope will be understood by my African American brothers and sisters. It is, I hope, a loving observation. Most of us would recognize that we have heard a sound of worship in black churches that we rarely hear anywhere else. The

sound of their laughter, Mary's laughter and that of my late friend
Dr. Ben Johnson, contains a unique quality I have seldom heard in
any other laughter. I call it "soul laughter." It resonates from a
heart that has known humiliation and yet transformed it into humility. So many hurtful experiences have been redeemed in the
echoes of that laughter. They are not laughing it off, but rather
laughing by means of a faith that acknowledges that what is hurtful is fleeting while the joy that is the foundation for the laughter
will last forever. It is a laugh of proud humility. I fed on it as a
child even as I am still feeding on the memory of it today.

Mary incarnated the truth that humble, loving servanthood
was the path to true strength of character, to an unimaginable
resiliency that served her till the end of her days. Though she was
humble and bore her humiliation with quiet nobility, no one was
ever less like a doormat than Mary Eddings. Her life was a lesson
lived out, not unlike the humiliating lesson of Jesus with his basin
and towel. I wonder if Jesus laughed his own "soul laugh" whenever he told the story of Peter and the footwashing.

No servant is greater than his master, no employee is greater
than her employer, as long as One lives and moves among us, bid-
ding us to wash each other's feet in sacramental language. The call
is not to become doormats. That would be a one-dimensional understanding of a much more complex call. It is a call to show the
world the full extent of our love by our willingness to wash feet
and perhaps even occasionally by refusing to wash windows.

14

The Death of a Slave

The Son of Man did not come to be served, but to serve, and to give His life—a ransom for many.

MATTHEW 20:28

IN CONTRAST TO THE AMBITION OF James and John, who sought thrones alongside their Rabbi, Jesus posits an unthinkable alternative. He, the *Kyrios*, has come to serve, not to be served. Masters bought slaves. Jesus, the Master, will give his life to purchase his servants. His life will be a ransom *(lytron)*, the price for the slave. Jesus will be the Master who pays the ransom for his slaves by dying as a slave. The cross as ransom provides the link. They are forever joined—slavery and salvation.

We all know that the cross was used as a form of capital punishment by the Romans. This was how criminals were executed. By law it was illegal for a Roman citizen to be crucified. This explains why tradition says Paul, who was a Roman citizen (Acts 22:25-28), was beheaded while Peter, who was not, was crucified. Cicero claims that even the thought of crucifixion should be put out of the mind of every citizen of Rome. But crucifixion (as well as flagellation) was viewed as a punishment reserved especially for slaves. In A.D. 61 a wealthy Roman named Secundus was murdered by one of his slaves. In an attempt to make a statement to other slaves, each one of his four hundred slaves was crucified.

In the *Bacchides*, the Roman playwright Plautus pictures a slave named Chrysalus (gold bearer) who is afraid that his master will change his name to Cruasalis (cross bearer). The slave laments, "I know that the cross will be my tomb: there laid my father, grandfather, great-grandfather."

A few days before the crucifixion of Jesus, Matthew records that Judas went to the high priest, asking, "What are you willing to give me if I hand Him over to you?" (26:15). At this point a decision had to be made by the religious leaders in regard to the "how much" of the betrayal. According to Matthew, they eventually arrived at the figure of thirty pieces of silver. They decided on the amount based on a verse that is buried in the minutiae of the Torah: "If the ox gores a male or female slave, he must give 30 shekels of silver to the slave's master, and the ox must be stoned" (Exodus 21:32).

The rabbis had determined from this verse that the base price for any slave, male or female, sick or well, would be thirty pieces of silver. I find it moving that when the discussion inevitably arose between Judas and the priests of how much was going to be paid for the betrayal of Jesus it was this obscure verse which provided the dark answer. Jesus was sold for the price of a slave. And in a matter of hours they hoped he would die like a slave; on a cross. Clearly Jesus would die *as* a slave, nailed to the cross beam, but he would not die *like* a slave.

Jesus had lived his life as their Servant Savior. When the disciples were hungry, he fed them. When their feet were dirty on the night of Judas' betrayal, he washed them. Perhaps it was Judas who decided that if he was going to act like a slave, instead of the Messiah, then he should be sold as one, maybe even die like one.

Perhaps of the Twelve, it was Judas who was the least willing to embrace both the call to become a slave as well as the servant image of his Master, Jesus.

In the midst of a slave culture, none of the disciples ever dreamed that the Messiah would come armed with a basin and a towel. When Jesus approached Peter at the Last Supper to wash his feet, such a thing was inappropriate, unthinkable; almost as unthinkable as a crucified man walking away from an empty tomb. But in his relentless response to Peter, "If you do not allow this then we have nothing in common," Jesus was making it clear: If you do not understand him as Servant, then you do not understand him at al—and you never will.

From the moment of the arrest in the garden, the image begins to take its final focus:

The Gospels tell us Jesus was bound. Slaves were bound. A *titulus*, a white gypsum-covered board accompanied him to the cross and was later hung over his head. It served as a description of him: "Jesus of Nazareth, King of the Jews." In the agora, gypsum-covered placards were hung around the necks of slaves describing where they were from and what skills they possessed. (This was also the practice in American slave markets.)

Before he begins his excruciating journey to the place of execution, Jesus is flogged with a *flagrum*, a scourging whip. Roman law dictated that a criminal would be flogged until "the flesh hung from his back." Everyday, all over the Roman world, slaves were flogged as a means of discipline. In one of his plays the writer Plautus says that slaves were "born to be thrashed." This was literally true in Jesus' case. For this he had been born, he says, for this he came into the world. (The most graphic accounts that come to us from the world of the African American slaves are those of brutal floggings.)

On the cross, when Jesus complains of his thirst, he is given sour wine ("wine vinegar") to drink. Cato the Elder, in his detailed instructions on the "care and feeding" of slaves says that they should be given the sour wine to drink.

The *titulus*, the *flagrum*, the sponge soaked in sour wine, the cross . . . these are the grim paraphernalia of slavery and crucifixion. Most often slaves were crucified for running away. They could be seen hanging on crosses, their foreheads branded with the letters *FUG* for *fugitivus*. This is where the analogy absolutely breaks down and ceases to be applicable. Jesus was not a fugitive. He was not running away from anything. He chose to live and die as the Servant Savior. Mysteriously, he chose to bear on his resurrected body forever the marks of crucifixion, the scars in his hands, feet and side. Slaves of every age have been recognized by such scars. But on Jesus there were not, nor could there ever have been any of the branded letters of the fugitive.

I struggle to imagine how I could possibly be worth the price of the ransom Jesus paid to purchase my freedom. The answer is I am clearly not worth it. But I am asking the wrong question. It is not, "What am I worth?" but rather, "What am I worth to him?"

15

Breakfast with
a Wounded Slave

AFTER THE RESURRECTION, JESUS appeared to the disciples
on the shore of the Lake of Galilee. They did not recognize him at
first as he stood there on the shore with his ruined hands, beside
a small coal fire about one hundred yards from where they were in
the boat. He asks them the irritating question, "You haven't caught
any fish, have you?" knowing they had been fishing all night long
with nothing to show for their labor. "Throw your nets to star-
board," he shouts. We all know the result.

After Peter jumps in and swims to shore, the disciples discover
that fish and bread are cooking on the fire. Jesus has prepared
breakfast for his disciples. There is nothing in the Gospels to keep
us from presuming that this might have been his habit. Perhaps he
fixed their breakfast most every morning. This touching image is
the parting picture of John's Gospel. John must have told this story
over and over again, since here, in chapter 21, it is his disciples
who are telling it for us. It is widely accepted that John's Gospel
comes to a conclusion at the end of chapter 20 and that chapter 21
was appended by his disciples to help explain a rumor that had
begun to spread after the death of John that reportedly said John
would not die until Jesus' return. For me the story of the early

morning miraculous catch provides the perfect backdrop for the song of the slave in Philippians 2.

The unrecognized One, standing on the shore, is unquestionably the Lord, the resurrected Jesus of Nazareth. His hands, feet and side still bear the marks of his slave's death. If you or I had contrived the story, Jesus would be standing there, in glory, surrounded by the legions of angels he earlier said he had at his command. As the disciples approached he would have invited them to fall on the rocky shore and worship him. This is what we would expect. This is the kind of glory we understand.

But we never get what we expect with Jesus. He is there, just as the song sings, in humility. He is serving the disciples. Even as he had washed their feet, now he performs the task of a slave. Precisely here the story becomes the perfect background for the ancient song that concludes:

> For this reason God also highly exalted Him
> and gave Him the name that is above every name,
> so that at the name of Jesus every knee should bow—
> of those who are in heaven and on earth and under the earth—
> and every tongue should confess that Jesus Christ is
>   Lord [kyrios]
> to the glory of God the Father. (Philippians 2:9-11)

To stand on the shore before the risen Savior, to see his ruined hands and realize that with them he has prepared one more meal for his disciples is to fall on our knees and worship him in a way we would have never imagined. Power, authority, glorious realms of angels—these are what we might have imagined or expected. Before them we would have contrived to bend the knee and mutter whatever words of worship we might make up. But to take in the sight of the humble wounded Master, standing beside the fire, is to be overcome with an appreciation of his unspeakable worth.

The unbroken chain of obedience that was his life, including this humbling moment, is why God has exalted him, because Jesus refused to exalt himself. This is why his name is above every name, because though he was the Lord and Master, he took on the title of a suffering slave. The radical reversal he lived out to perfection, the paradox the song celebrates, is precisely the nature of *Christos Kyrios,* Christ the Master.

16

Capture Me,
for I Am Fleeing

MY PREOCCUPATION WITH THE ISSUE of slavery in the Bible began with a small grainy black and white picture in a world history book. The image was of a metal disk of indeterminate size. The caption read: "A slave collar." Incised on the round tag were the words "Capture me, for I am fleeing." In both Rome and early America slaves were forced to wear such collars.

The more I meditated on the inscription on that tag, the clearer it became; those words could be engraved across my life, for in one way or another I am always fleeing. I flee God's compassion and what I sometimes perceive as his unreasonable demands, his grace, his command, his ownership over me, his embrace.

Perhaps that is why that small letter to Philemon on behalf of Onesimus the runaway slave was included in the writings of the New Testament. Most of us will never willingly conform to the Old Testament paradigm of the slave of the order of the pierced ear (Exodus 21:5-6). To be truthful, we are more like the runaway Onesimus, who while fleeing was captured or perhaps recaptured. Someone or something has to keep sending us back to our Master, to keep recapturing our imaginations so that we can appreciate the paradoxical freedom of slavery.

The fundamental fact of freedom is that it is always provided and made possible through the sacrifice of others. True freedom comes no other way.

"It is for freedom that Christ has set us free," Paul writes (Galatians 5:1 NIV). Jesus has provided the only true freedom, by the only legitimate means. He has purchased, ransomed, paid for us by the only legal tender that could perfectly cover the cost. His death purchased our lives in order that we might die in order that we might truly live. He sacrificed his freedom to set us free so that we might become slaves so that we might be truly free. The Master becomes the slave in order to become Master in the truest sense of the word. The slave to sin becomes free in order to become a slave of righteousness in order to become free in the truest sense of the word.

Aristotle says that the freeborn artisan or mechanic lives in a world of "separate slavery." He describes the futility of the life of a person who is owned by no one and only works to survive. This state is worse than slavery, says Aristotle, because this person lacks the identity of a Master. He is even more like an animal or an inanimate tool, a mere instrument of production. He does not participate in the Master's life. What is worse than being a slave? Being owned by no one.

When Jesus tells his disciples that he no longer calls them servants but friends (John 15:13-15), he means something like this. He is not saying their slavery is over. Otherwise Paul, Peter, James, Jude and John would not have continued to sign themselves as "slaves to Christ." What Jesus means is that they will possess a new identity, precisely because of their commitment to his Father as servants. Their servanthood, their slavery runs parallel to their friendship with the Father. It does not end with Jesus' pronouncement that they are friends. It only begins. It will become their dual identity. It will become the basis for their hope of hearing "Well done" upon the return of Jesus. It will provide sufficient reason for them to avoid complaining about and judging others. It will offer the only adequate model for the radical obedience, which is their only choice in following Jesus.

Without this perspective they will have nothing in common with Jesus. It alone will offer the clarity they will need. They will have only one Master to please, the *Kyrios* who purchased them with himself, who has enslaved them to set them free. They will live and serve and die within the confines of that first promise: "I will even pour out my Spirit on my . . . slaves" (Acts 2:18).

Ancient inscriptions reveal that two of the most popular slave names were Philodespotes and Philokyrios. Both could be translated "master lover." They were no doubt popular names because they were given *by* the masters to the slaves when they were newly purchased. I am still struggling with my identity as a slave of Christ. Nevertheless, I want to be known as Philokyrios, the Lover of the Master. I would proudly have that name inscribed on the slave's medallion around my neck, followed by the humbling phrase, "Capture me, for I am fleeing."

The freedom of slavery is a paradoxical freedom, just as the crucified life is a paradoxical living. The tension must be maintained—poverty for wealth, wisdom for foolishness, maturity as childlikeness, slavery for freedom.

The truth of who we are becoming in Christ is so vast that it forces us to make these seemingly contradictory statements. It is like trying to put your arms around an enormous building. I reach out with one hand and say, "I am a slave." I extend the other and affirm, "I am Jesus' intimate friend and coheir."

He places contradictory words in my mouth and has me say, "I

am only a worthless slave doing his duty." Then he reminds me
that I am of inestimable worth.

He commands and demands that I take up the cross and die. But
he frustratingly, infuriatingly says he has come to give me life.

This would all be unbearable and would eventually tear his followers apart except for the single undeniable fact that he perfectly
lived out the impossible paradox for us.

He surrendered to achieve victory.

He won everything by losing everything.

He died in order to live.

He washed feet, made breakfast, waited on, cared for, humbled
and humiliated himself in a thousand ways we will never know of
to forever establish himself as our unquestioned Master.

Epilogue

Freedom

I am lost and I am bound
I am captive to the shame
That keeps on holding me down
And all I need to be found
Is freedom

I am tired and I am dying
I am trapped inside a cage I made
Of hopelessly trying
But the door would open
And I'd be flying
If I could find freedom

Freedom Freedom
All the burdens we have borne
All the losses we have mourned
Cry out for freedom freedom

Prison walls and bolted doors
Something keeps on telling me

That I was made for more
That there is Someone
Who could restore
My freedom
A gentle voice I can't evade
Speaks in the darkness of the heart
And whispers, "Do not be afraid"
You can be free, the price was paid
For your freedom

Freedom Freedom
From the darkness of the night
From desolation to delight
Freedom Freedom
The chains are broken
The door is open
He is your freedom

(Words and music by Michael Card are available for free download at <michaelcard.com>, as well as additional lectures on slavery in the New Testament.)

Coda

by Sara Groves

If mercy should be shown anywhere, says Jesus' story, it should be shown between people who know themselves to be slaves.

MICHAEL CARD

IN THESE PAGES WE HAVE BEEN INVITED to reimagine the life of a slave through the lens of Roman and American history. But we don't have to go back in time to face the brutality of slavery. At 27 million, there are more slaves today than there were in 400 years of the transatlantic slave trade.

A few years ago I had the opportunity to meet a young woman while she was giving her testimony in Washington, D.C. Elizabeth was the oldest of seven children from a Christian family living in Southeast Asia. Between her sophomore and junior years in high school, she sought a job to help her save money for Bible college. A trusted woman in the community offered to travel with her to a neighboring town where she knew of a job opportunity. But once they were out of sight of their hometown, the woman turned on her and sold her to a human trafficker. The trafficker sold her to a brothel owner.

At 15 years of age, Elizabeth found herself in a brothel in a foreign country, subjected to horrible abuse. She prayed every night that God would rescue her, even as the other girls in the brothel mocked her and told her God could not hear her. When she gave her testimony to those gathered in Washington, she simply said, "Still I believed."

For months Elizabeth was forced to work at the brothel. Then an International Justice Mission operative found Elizabeth. IJM is a human rights agency that secures justice for victims of slavery, sexual exploitation and other forms of violent oppression. IJM lawyers, investigators and aftercare professionals work with local officials to ensure immediate victim rescue and aftercare, to prosecute perpetrators and to promote functioning public justice systems.

That day they rescued Elizabeth and other girls held against their will. When they went in to gather Elizabeth's belongings, they found Psalm 27 written on the wall above her mattress: "The Lord is my light and my salvation. Whom shall I fear? The Lord is the stronghold of my life. Of whom shall I be afraid?"

Elizabeth has now graduated from college and is working in ministry as a translator. She tells her story so that other girls will be saved from this brutality. Her faith and courage ask me a question, and have led me to life-changing conclusions. Because of the generosity of Christ to come find me in my sin and suffering, I am compelled to enter into the suffering of others.

If you are interested in learning more about the work to end modern-day slavery, please visit <www.ijm.org>.

Appendix A

A Comparison of the Three Worlds of Slavery

OLD TESTAMENT SLAVERY

1. "Slave of the LORD" was a title of honor (Moses, Joshua 14:7; Joshua, Judges 2:8; Abraham, Psalm 105:42; David, Psalm 89:3).

2. Slavery was a part of the national identity (Exodus 13:3; 20:2; Leviticus 25:55).

3. Slavery played only a minor role in the economic life of Israel. The norm seems to have been small-scale, indentured household slavery.

4. Slaves were given the provision of sabbath rest (Exodus 20:10; Deuteronomy 5:14).

5. The Law protected them from various types of abuse (Exodus 21:20-21; Deuteronomy 23:15-16).

6. Hebrew slaves were to be released in the Jubilee year (Leviticus 25:39-43). (There is no record of the Jubilee ever being observed.)

7. Indentured Hebrew slaves were released after six years (Exodus 21:1-11; Deuteronomy 15:12-18; see Jeremiah 34:8-17 for a violation of this law). Gentiles were slaves for life (Leviticus 25:44-46).

8. A Hebrew slave could be redeemed by a "kinsman redeemer" or an alien (Leviticus 25:47-55).

9. A Hebrew slave could redeem himself.

10. After working off a debt, provision was made for the freed slave to make a fresh start with his own stock.

11. The base price for a slave was thirty pieces of silver (Exodus 21:32).

12. Special protection was extended to female slaves, protecting their marital status (Deuteronomy 21:10-14). Captured women could be taken as wives, not slaves. If divorced they could not become slaves.

13. Slaves were protected from being killed by their masters (Exodus 21:20; Leviticus 24:17, 22).

14. Special protection was mandated for runaway slaves (Deuteronomy 23:15).

15. An injured slave was to be set free (Exodus 21:26).

16. Slaves would not necessarily stand out by virtue of race or dress.

17. In the history of Israel there was never a movement to abolish slavery.

18. Slaves could choose to become slaves for life (Exodus 21:6).

WAYS TO BECOME A SLAVE

1. Prisoner of war (Genesis 14:21; Numbers 31:9; Deuteronomy 20:14; 2 Kings 5:2)

2. By purchase (Genesis 17:12; Ecclesiastes 2:7)

3. By birth, "houseborn slaves" (Genesis 15:3; 17:12-13; Jeremiah 2:14)

4. For restitution, as a means for a thief to make good on damages (Exodus 22:3)

5. To pay off a debt (Exodus 21:2-6, 7-11; Deuteronomy 15:18; 2 Kings 4:1)

6. Kidnapping, which was a capital offense (Exodus 21:16; Deuteronomy 24:7)

WAYS TO FREEDOM

1. The Sabbatical Year (Exodus 21; Deuteronomy 15)

2. Jubilee (Leviticus 25:13)

3. A woman whose master refused marriage (Exodus 21:7-11)

4. Purchase by a "kinsman redeemer" (Leviticus 25)

5. As the result of an injury (Exodus 21:26-27)

Examples: Jacob, slave to Laban (Genesis 29:18); Joseph sold to Midianites (Genesis 37:36; 39:1); David enslaves Ammonites (2 Samuel 12:31); temple slaves (Joshua 9:3-27)

SLAVERY IN THE NEW TESTAMENT ERA

1. Slaves were despised. To call someone a "slave" was a serious insult. Cato the Elder wrote, "He who has a slave has an enemy." See John 8:33.

2. Slaves played a major role in the economic world. The Roman Empire was dependent on slavery.

3. In general slaves had no rights. In the earlier Republic this was literally true. But in the time of the Empire, the New Testament era, some laws were written to give marginal protection, though they were often not enforced. Slaves could be killed or mutilated by their owners.

4. Slaves left virtually no "voice" in the ancient records. We only

have playwrights like Plautus and Petronius who caricature and ridicule slaves.

5. Slaves were often manumitted or could even purchase their own freedom from their own savings (*peculium*). Exceptions were agricultural and mining slaves, who represent the vast majority of slaves, who were never freed.

6. Slavery could present a chance for upward mobility. But this opportunity was limited to an extremely small percentage. It was better to be the slave of an influential person than to simply be free and poor.

7. Education enhanced the value of a slave and so was encouraged among house slaves.

8. Paternity among slaves was virtually never recognized.

9. Prices for slaves varied widely. A doctor was worth fifty times a farm worker.

10. Sexual abuse was common and taken for granted. Half of female slaves died before age thirty.

11. Slaves could own property, even other slaves. But their possessions were still under the control of their masters, even if they became freedmen.

12. Provision for the average slave was meager. Cato speaks of a new cloak and shoes every two years. Archeologists have never verified sleeping quarters for slaves.

13. Runaways were frequent, an obsession in the ancient records. Roman law forbade the sheltering of runaways. Professional "slave catchers" captured fugitives. Runaway slaves were branded, mutilated and fitted with iron collars that were

sometimes inscribed with the words, "Capture me for I am fleeing."

14. There was never a movement to abolish slavery, though there were several slave revolts, such as Spartacus in 73-71 B.C.

15. Roman slavery was not race-based. Slaves were virtually indistinguishable by dress or race. (Exception: Some races were preferred for certain jobs, such as Gauls and Germanics for farming/mines and Greeks for more professional tasks.)

Sources for Slaves

1. Captives in battle ("The most just means," said Dionysius of Halicarnassus) and piracy

2. Kidnapping

3. Rescue of "exposed" infants

4. Penal slaves

5. International slave trade

6. Reproduction

African American Slavery

It is difficult to generalize concerning American slavery since laws and regulations differed from state to state. Often plantations located next to each other treated slaves in radically different ways. For example, on one plantation slaves would be whipped for praying or singing while down the road others might be whipped for not attending church.

1. Slaves were despised.

2. Slavery was basic to the economy.

3. Slaves were often given the sabbath to rest.

4. Laws to protect them from abuse were usually ignored. They effectively had no rights.

5. We have several eloquent voices preserved in slave literature and narratives, such as Frederick Douglass, Booker T. Washington and Olaudah Equiano.

6. Slaves were sometimes manumitted, usually upon the death of their owners. There are a few rare examples of individuals purchasing their own freedom.

7. Education was seen as a threat and was eventually made illegal.

8. Paternity was not recognized. Few slaves knew who their fathers were. Douglass mentions that he knew of no slaves who knew their birthday.

9. Sexual abuse was common, virtually a part of the system.

10. Rarely slaves might own property.

11. Provision was poor, especially for children. Douglass describes children, usually naked, eating boiled corn meal from troughs on the ground.

12. Eventually an abolitionist movement led to the end of slavery.

13. Runaways were common. Those captured were branded and otherwise mutilated. Patrols of "slave catchers" were common.

14. American slavery was race-based.

SOURCES FOR SLAVES

1. Kidnapping/slave trade

2. Natural reproduction (after the closure of the slave trade in 1809 the slave population went up 33 percent in the South)

3. Some prisoners of war

Appendix B

A Lexicon of Slavery

apostolos. Someone sent, an emissary, a messenger (perhaps a slave) sent with the imputed authority of another, someone who is commissioned for a task (Luke 6:13; John 13:16; Acts 4:33; 2 Corinthians 8:23). Often used in parallel with *doulos* (John 13:16; Romans 1:1; Titus 1:1; 2 Peter 1:1).

anthropareskoi. "People-pleasers" (Ephesians 6:6; Colossians 3:22).

apolytrosis. Buying back a slave, release, redemption (Luke 21:28; Romans 8:24; Ephesians 1:7, 14; Colossians 1:14; Hebrews 9:15).

diakonos. Servant, one who is in the service of a master (Matthew 20:26; 22:13; Acts 6:2-6; Romans 16:1; Philippians 1:1; 1 Timothy 3:8-13). Note that Luke, the former slave, does not use this word.

despotes. Master, owner (Acts 4:24; 1 Timothy 6:1-2; 2 Peter 2:1; Jude 4; Revelation 6:10).

dikaioo. To show justice, to be pronounced righteous, to be set free (Matthew 12:37; Acts 13:39; Romans 3:24, 26, 28, 30; 5:9; 1 Corinthians 6:11; Titus 3:7).

doulos. Slave, someone who belongs to another (Matthew 10:24; 20:27; Mark 10:44; 12:46; 19:17; John 13:16; 15:15, 20; Romans 1:1; 1 Corinthians 7:22; 2 Corinthians 4:5; Ephesians 6:6; 2 Timothy 2:24; James 1:1; 2 Peter 1:1; Jude 1; also *syndoulos*, "fellow slave").

ebed. Primary Hebrew word for "slave" or "servant." From *abad*, to work. Occurs 799 times in the Old Testament.

exagorazo. Redeem, to buy from the marketplace (Galatians 3:13; 4:5; Ephesians 5:16).

hyperetes. One who serves a master or superior, assistant (Luke 1:2; John 18:36; 1 Corinthians 4:1)

katakrima. Condemnation as penal servitude (Romans 5:16, 18; 8:1).

katallage. Reconcilation (Romans 5:11; 11:15; 2 Corinthians 5:18, 19).

kyrios. Master, owner, a title of sovereignty (Matthew 6:24; 10:24; 21:40; 24:50; 25:21; Mark 7:28; 13:35; Luke 12:42-47; John 13:13; Colossians 4:1; often used as the Greek translation of the Hebrew word *adon*).

lytron. The ransom for a slave, a sum of money paid out to buy back a slave (Matthew 20:28; Mark 10:45).

misthios. Wage earner, in contrast to the slave (Luke 15:17, 19).

oiketes. House slave (Luke 16:13; Acts 10:7; Romans 14:4; 1 Peter 2:18).

ophthalmodoulia. "Eye-slavery" (Ephesians 6:6; Colossians 3:22).

paidagogos. A slave who tends a child (1 Corinthians 4:15; Galatians 3:24, 25).

pais. "Boy slave" (Matthew 8:6-13; 12:18; Luke 1:54; Acts 3:13; 4:27). Slaves would be referred to as "boys" well past the Jim Crow days in America.

peculium. A Latin term for the "assets a slave was allowed to accumulate which were still ultimately under the control of the master." (Not found in the New Testament.)

philodespotes. "Master lover," a popular slave name. (Not found in the New Testament.)

philokyrios. "Master lover," a popular slave name, traditionally given by the master. (Not found in the New Testament.)

tapeinophrosyne. Lowliness of mind, humility (Acts 20:19; Ephesians 4:2; Philippians 2:3; Colossians 2:18, 23; 3:12; 1 Peter 5:5). Considered the posture of a slave.

therapon. A personal attendant, used to describe Moses in Hebrews 3:5. Also *therapeia* in Luke 12:42, a group of personal slaves.

SOURCES

Arndt, William, and F. Wilbur Gingrich. *A Greek-English Lexicon of the New Testament.* Chicago: University of Chicago Press, 1957.

Hornblower, Simon, and Anthony Spawforth. *The Oxford Classical Dictionary.* Oxford: Oxford University Press, 1999.

Kittel, Gerhard, and Gerhard Friedrich, eds. *Theological Dictionary of the New Testament.* 10 vols. Grand Rapids: Eerdmans, 1964-1976.

McReynolds, Paul R. *Word Study Greek-English New Testament.* Wheaton: Tyndale House, 1990.

Xavier, Leon-Dufour. *Dictionary of the New Testament.* San Francisco: Harper and Row, 1983.

Appendix C

A List of Possible Slaves in the New Testament

Determining slave names is not an exact science. In the list below some identify themselves as "slaves of Christ," while others are definitively identified as literal slaves. A few on the list are conjectured to be likely slaves because of their names.

1. Jesus, Acts 3:13, 26; Romans 15:8; Philippians 2:7

2 Mary, "I am the Lord's slave," Luke 1:38

3. The slave of the Roman officer, Luke 7:2

4. The slave girl in the courtyard, Matthew 26:69

5. Malchus, John 18:10

6. Joseph, Acts 7:9

7. David, Acts 4:25

8. Hagar, Galatians 4:25

9. Moses, Hebrews 3:5; Revelation 15:3

10. Paul, a slave of God, Romans 1:1; Ephesians 3:7; Titus 1:1

11. Luke

12. James, a slave of God, James 1:1

13. Simon Peter, a slave and apostle of Jesus Christ, 2 Peter 1:1

14. John, Revelation 1:1

15. Jude, a slave of Jesus Christ, Jude 1

16. Rhoda, Acts 12:13

17. Blastus, Acts 12:20

18. Phoebe, Romans 16:1

19. Tychicus, Ephesians 6:21

20. Epaphras, Colossians 4:12

21. An angel, Revelation 19:10; 22:9

22. Felix (former slave of Claudius), Acts 24:22

23. Andronicus, Romans 16:7

24. Urbanus, Romans 16:9

25. Aristarchus, Acts 19:29; 20:4; 27:2; Colossians 4:10; Philemon 24

26. Rufus, Mark 15:21; Romans 16:13

27. Household of Aristobulus, Romans 16:10; household of Narcissus, Romans 16:11

28. Onesimus, Philemon

Appendix D

The Slave Parables

The Unforgiving Slave, Matthew 18:23-35

The Wicked House Slave, Matthew 21:33-46; Mark 12:1-12;
    Luke 20:9-19

The Wicked Slave, Matthew 24:45-51; Luke 12:42-48

"Well Done," Matthew 25:14-30

The Watchful Slave, Mark 13:33-37

The Two Debtors, Luke 7:41-47

The Good Samaritan Who Serves as a Slave, Luke 10:30-37

The Faithful Slave, Luke 12:35-40

The Feast Invitations, Luke 14:12-14

The Older Slaving Brother, Luke 15:11-32

The Unjust Steward, Luke 16:1-9

"No Slave Can Have Two Masters," Luke 16:13

The Master and Slaves, Luke 17:7-10

Slaves to Sin, John 8:34 (see also Romans 7:23-25)

Appendix E

The Facts of Modern Slavery

- Human trafficking is the world's third largest criminal enterprise, after drugs and weapons.

- Worldwide, there are nearly two million children in the commercial sex trade.

- An estimated 600,000 to 800,000 children, women and men are trafficked across international borders annually.

- Approximately 80 percent of human trafficking victims are women and girls, and up to 50 percent are minors.

- The total market value of illicit human trafficking is estimated to be in excess of $32 billion.

- Sex trafficking is an engine of the global AIDS epidemic.

Bonded slavery is the continual labor of an individual forced to work by mental or physical threat. Bonded slaves are owned by an employer to whom the slave or slave's family is indebted. Bonded slaves are forced to work long hours, often seven days a week, for meager wages, if any, attempting to pay back a debt that increases at exorbitant interest rates. In reality, there is no way to repay the debt and the laborer essentially becomes a slave for life. Many bonded slaves are children who are beaten and abused if they do not fulfill the extreme expectations of the owner.

What are the facts?

- According to the United Nations Working Group on Contemporary Forms of Slavery, an estimated 20 million people were held in bonded slavery as of 1999.

- In 2004 there are more slaves than were seized from Africa during four centuries of transatlantic slave trade.

- In 1850 a slave in the Southern United States cost the equivalent of $40,000 today. According to Free the Slaves, a slave today costs an average of $90.

- Approximately two-thirds of today's slaves are in South Asia. Human Rights Watch estimates that in India alone there are as many as 15 million children in bonded slavery.

How does bonded slavery happen?

When a personal or family emergency requires immediate funds the individual or family is forced to work for very little or no pay in exchange for a small loan. Because the debt increases faster than they're paid a slave is trapped without hope of ever paying off the original debt. While IJM does not often find victims in physical chains, the intimidation of powerful oppressors is every bit as effective a means of restraint.

(Source, International Justice Mission)

For more information go to <www.ijm.org>.

Notes

Introduction

p. 11   "There the conviction": Simone Weil, *Wrestling with God* (McLean, Va.: The Trinity Forum, 2008), p. 11.

p. 13   when William Lane looked: For more about our friendship, see Michael Card, *The Walk: The Life-Changing Journey of Two Friends* (Grand Rapids: Discovery House, 2006).

Chapter 2: A Better Freedom

p. 21   "But let slaves serve": Jack N. Sparks, *The Apostolic Fathers* (Minneapolis: Light and Life, 1978).

Chapter 3: One Word, Three Worlds

p. 27   "the most prominent personal": R. Laird Harris, *Theological Wordbook of the Old Testament* (Chicago: Moody Press, 1980), 2:639.

p. 28   "It is singularly monstrous": Simone Weil, *Wrestling with God* (McLean, Va.: The Trinity Forum, 2008), p. 12.

p. 29   "the most just means": Dionysius of Halicarnassus *Roman Antiquities* 4.24.2, trans. Earnest Cary, Loeb Classical Library (Cambridge, Mass.: Harvard University Press, 1939).

p. 30   They are often touching examples: See Brian K. Harvey, *Roman Lives: Ancient Roman Life as Illustrated by Latin Inscriptions* (Newburyport, Mass.: Focus Classical Sources, 2004).

p. 30   Cato speaks of a new cloak: Cato and Varro *On Agriculture*, trans. W. D. Hooper, Loeb Classical Library (Cambridge, Mass.: Harvard University Press), pp. 56-59.

p. 32   ex-slave Reverend Thomas Jones referred: In William L. Andrews, ed., *North Carolina Slave Narratives* (Chapel Hill: University of North Carolina Press, 2003), p. 214.

Chapter 5: My Son, Onesimus

pp. 46-47   letter to Sabinianus: Pliny the Younger. *Letters,* trans. William
            Melmoth, rev. F. C. T. Bosanquet, The Harvard Classics (New
            York: P. F. Collier & Son, 1909-1914), 9.4.

p. 48   Thomas X. Sims letter: John W. Blassingame, *Slave Testimony;
            Two Centuries of Letters, Speeches, Interviews* (Baton Rouge:
            Louisiana State University Press, 1977), pp. 91-92.

Chapter 6: Eye-Slaves and People-Pleasers

pp. 55-56   Lunsford Lane: Excerpts from William L. Andrews, ed., *North
            Carolina Slave Narratives* (Chapel Hill: University of North
            Carolina Press, 2003), p. 109.

p. 57   Plato said, "A man should": Plato, *Phaedrus,* ed. Mortimer
            Adler, Great Books of the Western World (Chicago: Encyclo-
            pedia Britannica, 1952), p. 274.

Chapter 8: Don't Worry About It

p. 66   "For a believer ought not": *Apostolic Consitutions* 2.7.62; *Ante-
            Nicene Fathers,* ed. Alexander Roberts, James Donaldson and
            A. Cleveland Coxe, trans. James Donaldson (1886; reprint,
            Peabody, Mass.: Hendrickson, 1994), 7:424.

Chapter 9: Freed From and Freed To

pp. 69-70   Douglass says . . . "disgust their slaves with freedom": Henry
            Louis Gates, *The Classic Slave Narratives* (New York: Signet,
            2002), p. 397.

Chapter 10: Christ the Slave

p. 80   "They gather early in the morning": Pliny the Younger, *Letters
            and Panegyricus,* I, Books 1-7, trans. Betty Radice, Loeb Clas-
            sical Library (Cambridge, Mass.: Harvard University Press,
            1969), Ep. 10.96.4-5.

p. 80   When Harriet Tubman: Sarah Bradford, *Scenes in the Life of
            Harriet Tubman* (Freeport, N.Y.: Books for Libraries Press,
            1971), p. 20.

p. 80   340 years of slavery: The first African American slaves came
             to the New World aboard a Dutch pirate ship in 1619, landing
             near Jamestown, Virginia. See Kai Wright, *The African Ameri-
             can Archive: The History of the Black Experience Through Docu-
             ments* (New York: Black Dog and Leventhal, 2001), p. 4.

p. 81   "If any slave": From Petronius's *Satyricon* in Basil Davenport,
             The Portable Roman Reader (New York: Penguin, 1951), p.
             534.

p. 82   "The cheerful spark that lingered": Henry Louis Gates, *The
             Classic Slave Narratives* (New York: Signet, 2002), p. 386.

p. 82   Crucifixion . . . was seen as a slave's death: Tacitus, *Histories*,
             4.11, quoted by Murray J. Harris, *Slave of Christ* (Downers
             Grove, Ill.: InterVarsity Press, 1999), p. 43.

Chapter 11: Slaves Who Waited for the Way

p. 85   "All night long they must stand": Seneca, *Moral Letters* 47
             quoted by Jennifer Glancy, *Slavery in Early Christianity* (Min-
             neapolis: Fortress, 2006), p. 137.

p. 85   Frederick Douglass tells a story: Henry Louis Gates, *The Clas-
             sic Slave Narratives* (New York: Signet, 2002), p. 357.

p. 87   "We sang the most": Gates, *Classic Slave Narratives*, p. 350.

p. 88   "I know why the caged bird sings": *The Complete Poems of Paul
             Laurence Dunbar* (New York: Dodd, Mead, 1922), p. 102.

p. 93   "All services which a slave does": TB Ketuboth 96a quoted in
             William Lane, *The Gospel According to Mark*, The New Inter-
             national Commentary on the New Testament (Grand Rapids:
             Eerdmans, 1974), p. 52.

Chapter 12: Parables of Slavery

p. 115   Frederick Douglass's remembrance: Henry Louis Gates, *The
             Classic Slave Narratives* (New York: Signet, 2002), p. 363.

Chapter 13: The Servant Savior

p. 122   a free person acting as a slave: Josephus, *Antiquities of the Jews*

(Grand Rapids: Kregel, 1960), 4.6.11.

Chapter 14: The Death of a Slave

p. 128   "I know that the cross": Plautus, *The Two Bacchides*, trans. Paul Nixon, Loeb Classical Library (Cambridge Mass.: Harvard University Press, 1916), p. 362.

p. 129   In one of his plays: Plautus, *Pseudolus* Act 1, sc 2. quoted in Jon E. Lewis, *The Mammoth Book of Eyewitness Ancient Rome* (New York: Carrol and Graf, 2003), p. 32.

Chapter 16: Capture Me, for I Am Fleeing

p. 136   Aristotle says that: Aristotle, *Great Ideas: Syntopicon II,* ed. Mortimer Adler, The Great Books of the Western World (Chicago: Encyclopedia Britannica, 1952), p. 777.

Bibliography

First-Century Slavery

Balsdon, J. P. V. D. *Life and Leisure in Ancient Rome.* London: Phoenix Press, 2002.

Banks, Robert. *Paul's Idea of Community.* Peabody, Mass.: Hendrickson, 1994.

Barrett, C. K. *The New Testament Background: Selected Documents.* New York: Harper and Row, 1956.

Bell, Albert A. *Exploring the New Testament World.* Nashville: Thomas Nelson, 1998.

Bruce, F. F. *New Testament History.* New York: Doubleday-Galilee, 1980.

Chadwick, Henry. *The Penguin History of the Church: The Early Church.* Vol 1. London: Penguin Books, 1967.

Charlesworth, James H., and Loren L. Johns. *Hillel and Jesus.* Minneapolis: Fortress, 1997.

Connolly, Peter. *Living in the Time of Jesus of Nazareth.* Bnei Brak: Steimatzky, 1988.

Cornfield, Gaalya, general ed. *Josephus: The Jewish War.* Grand Rapids: Zondervan, 1982.

Dowley, Tim, ed. *Introduction to the History of Christianity.* Minneapolis: Fortress, 1995.

Edersheim, Alfred. *Sketches of Jewish Social Life.* Grand Rapids: Eerdmans, 1979.

Ferguson, Everett. *Early Christians Speak.* Abilene, Tex.: Abilene Christian University Press, 1981.

Garnesy, Peter. *Ideas of Slavery from Aristotle to Augustine.* Cambridge: Cambridge University Press, 1996.

Glancy, Jennifer A. *Slavery in Early Christianity.* Minneapolis: Fortress, 2006.

Grant, Frederick. *Ancient Roman Religion*. Indianapolis: Bobbs-Merrill Educational Publishing, 1957.

————. *Hellenistic Religions*. Indianapolis: Bobbs-Merrill Educational Publishing, 1953.

Grant, Michael. *The Jews in the Roman World*. New York: Barnes and Noble, 1973.

Harris, Murray J. *Slave of Christ: A New Testament Metaphor for Total Devotion to Christ*. Downers Grove, Ill.: InterVarsity Press, 1999.

Harris, R. Laird. *Theological Wordbook of the Old Testament*, vol. 2. Chicago: Moody Press, 1980.

Harvey, Brian K. *Roman Lives: Ancient Roman Life as Illustrated by Latin Inscriptions*. Newburyport, Mass.: Focus Classical Sources, 2004.

Haywood, John. *Historical Atlas of the Classical World 500 BC to AD 600*. New York: Barnes and Noble, 2000.

Jeffers, James S. *The Greco-Roman World of the New Testament Era*. Downers Grove, Ill.: InterVarsity Press, 1999.

Keppie, Lawrence. *Understanding Roman Inscriptions*. Baltimore: Johns Hopkins University Press, 1991.

Kittel, Gerhard, and Gerhard Friedrich, eds. *Theological Dictionary of the New Testament*. 10 vols. Grand Rapids: Eerdmans, 1964-1976.

Lewis, Jon E. *The Mammoth Book of Eyewitness: Ancient Rome*. New York: Carroll and Graf, 2003.

Lohse, Eduard. *The New Testament Environment*. Nashville: Abingdon, 1993.

Maier, Paul L. *Eusebius: The Church History*. Grand Rapids: Kregel, 1999.

Martin, Dale B. *Slavery as Salvation*. New Haven: Yale University Press, 1990.

Matthews, Victor H. *Manners and Customs in the Bible*. Peabody, Mass.: Hendrickson, 1988.

McReynolds, Paul R. *Word Study Greek-English New Testament*. Wheaton, Ill.: Tyndale House, 1990.

Meeks, Wayne A., *The First Urban Christians*. New Haven: Yale University Press, 1983.

Millard, Alan. *Discoveries from the Times of Jesus*. Oxford: Lion, 1990.

————. *Nelson's Illustrated Wonders and Discoveries of the Bible*. Nashville: Thomas Nelson, 1997.

Pelikan, Jaroslav. *Jesus Through the Centuries*. New Haven: Yale University Press, 1999.

Plutarch. *The Lives of the Noble Grecians and Romans*. New York: Modern Library, 1992.

Saldarini, Anthony J. *Pharisees, Scribes and Sadducees in Palestinian Society*. Grand Rapids: Eerdmans, 2001.

Scheidel, Walter. *The Roman Slave Supply*. Princeton/Stanford Working Papers in Classics. Stanford University, May 2007.

Schürer, Emil. *A History of the Jewish People in the Time of Jesus*. New York: Schocken Books, 1978.

Stambaugh, John E., and David L. Balch. *The New Testament in Its Social Environment*. Philadelphia: Westminster Press, 1986.

Suetonius. *The Twelve Caesars,* translated by Michael Grant. London: Penguin, 1989.

Tacitus. *The Annals of Rome,* translated with an introduction by Michael Grant. London: Penguin, 1996.

Trapp, Leo. *Judaism: Development and Life*. Encino, Calif.: Dickenson, 1974.

Van Deursen, A. *Illustrated Dictionary of Bible Manners and Customs*. New York: Philosophical Library, 1982.

Walker, Peter. *Jesus and His World*. Downers Grove, Ill.: InterVarsity Press, 2003.

Westermann, William L. *The Slave Systems of Greek and Roman Antiquity*. Philadelphia: American Philosophical Society, 1955.

Wilken, Robert, *The Christians as the Romans Saw Them*. New Haven: Yale University Press, 1984.

Zeitlin, Irving M. *Jesus and the Judaism of His Time*. Cambridge: Polity Press, 1988.

African American Slavery

Andrews, William L., ed. *North Carolina Slave Narratives*. Chapel Hill: University of North Carolina Press, 2003.

Berry, Wendell. *The Hidden Wound*. New York: North Point Press, 1989.

Blassingame, John W. *Slave Testimony: Two Centuries of Letters, Speeches, Interviews, and Autobiographies.* Baton Rouge: Louisiana State University Press, 1977.

Blight, David W. *A Slave No More: Two Men Who Escaped to Freedom.* Orlando: Harcourt, 2007.

Douglass, Frederick. *Narrative of the Life of Frederick Douglass, an American Slave.* Cornell University Library Digital Collections, 1992 (library.cornell.edu).

Du Bois, W. E. B. *The Souls of Black Folk.* New York: Bantam Books, 1989.

Gates, Henry Louis. *The Classic Slave Narratives.* New York: Signet, 2002.

Genovese, Eugene D. *Roll Jordan Roll: The World the Slaves Made.* New York: Vintage, 1972.

Howell, Donna Wyant. *I Was a Slave: True Life Stories Dictated by Former Slaves in the 1930's.* Washington, D.C.: American Legacy Books, 1995.

Johnson, Walter. *Soul by Soul: Life Inside the Antebellum Slave Market.* Cambridge, Mass.: Harvard University Press, 1999.

Jones, Arthur C. *Wade in the Water: The Wisdom of the Spirituals.* Maryknoll, N.Y.: Orbis, 1993.

Porter, Dorothy. *Early Negro Writing.* Baltimore: Black Classic Press, 1995.

Raboteau, Albert J. *Slave Religion: The "Invisible Institution" in the Antebellum South.* Oxford: Oxford University Press, 1978.

Ward, Andrew. *The Slave's War: The Civil War in the Words of Former Slaves.* Boston: Houghton Mifflin, 2008.

Washington, Booker T. *Up from Slavery: An American Autobiography.* New York: Bantam Books, 1956.

Weil, Simone. *Wrestling with God.* McLean, Va.: Trinity Forum, 2008.

Wright, Kai. *The African American Archive: The History of the Black Experience Through Documents.* New York: Black Dog and Leventhal, 2001.

There are numerous sources on the Internet. One of the best is

Eddie Becker's website on slavery, <innercity.org/holt/slavechron. html>. Also see the National Slavery Museum's site at </www.us nationalslaverymuseum.org>. Audible.com has downloadable versions of the works of Booker T. Washington and Frederick Douglass as well as *The Slave's War* and *A Slave No More*.

About the Author

Michael Card is a musician, performing artist and writer of "El Shaddai," "Immanuel" and many other songs. He has produced twenty-three albums. He has also written numerous books, including *Scribbling in the Sand, A Fragile Stone, A Sacred Sorrow, A Violent Grace, The Parable of Joy* and *Sleep Sound in Jesus* (a children's book). A graduate of Western Kentucky University with a bachelor's and master's degrees in biblical studies, Card was awarded an honorary Ph.D. in Christian education by Philadelphia Biblical University. He also serves as mentor to many younger artists and musicians, teaching courses on the creative process and calling the Christian recording industry into deeper discipleship. Card lives in Tennessee with his wife and four children.

Michael Card Music, LLC
P.O. Box 586
Franklin TN 37065-0586
Phone: 615/790-7675
info@michaelcard.com
www.michaelcard.com

Available from InterVarsity Press:
Scribbling in the Sand: Christ and Creativity
168 pages, paperback, ISBN: 978-0-8308-3254-5

A Fragile Stone: The Emotional Life of Simon Peter
192 pages, paperback, ISBN: 978-0-8308-3445-7

Joy in the Journey Through the Year
327 pages, paperback, ISBN: 978-0-8308-3295-8